Making things work

Making things work
An introduction to design technology

Ken Shooter

Inspector for Design and Technology, Cambridgeshire

and

John Saxton

Assessment of Performance Unit, Goldsmiths College, London

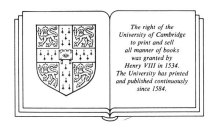

The right of the
University of Cambridge
to print and sell
all manner of books
was granted by
Henry VIII in 1534.
The University has printed
and published continuously
since 1584.

Cambridge University Press
Cambridge
New York   New Rochelle   Melbourne   Sydney

Published by the Press Syndicate of the University of Cambridge
The Pitt Building, Trumpington Street, Cambridge CB2 1RP
32 East 57th Street, New York, NY 10022, USA
10 Stamford Road, Oakleigh, Melbourne 3166, Australia

First published 1987

Printed in Great Britain by Scotprint Ltd, Musselburgh, Scotland

British Library cataloguing in publication data
Shooter, Ken
    Making things work: an introduction to
    design technology.
    1. Technology
    I. Title   II. Saxton, John
    600   T47

ISBN 0 521 33970 7

Cover design by Neil Sutton
Illustrated by John Plumb and D P Press
DP

Acknowledgements

The publishers would like to thank the following for permission to
reproduce their photographs:
the Cement and Concrete Association p38 (building with crane), p49;
Freeman Fox Ltd p53; Griffin and George p38 (skeleton); ZEFA (U.K.)
Ltd p82 and cover photograph.

The publishers would like to thank the following people for taking
photographs:
Charlotte Attwood p14 (circuit board), p72, p74, (pillar drill); Nick D
Brown p29, p38 (car, leaf, frame building, egg), p48, p50, p74 (BR
overhead cables system, car fan belt); Nigel Luckhurst p13, p17.

Contents

Introduction   1

Part 1 Energy   2

1 Energy: what is it?   2

2 Making your model more efficient   5

3 Work and power   9

Part 2 Electronics   13

1 Electricity: what is it?   13

2 Looking at circuits   17

3 Resistance and resistors   20

4 Using transistors   26

5 Capacitors and diodes   32

Part 3 Structures   38

1 Structures and forces   39

2 Columns and beams   42

3 Frameworks   48

4 Spanning gaps 51

5 Forces acting in a structure   54

Part 4 Mechanisms   60

1 Levers   62

2 Linkages   69

3 Pulleys and sprockets   72

4 Gears and gear mechanisms   76

Appendix 1 Electronics baseboard   85

Appendix 2 Component sources   86

Appendix 3 Basic electronics kit check list   87

Further reading   88

Note for teachers

Introduction

The aim of this book is to introduce young people to the practical problem solving world of design and technology in a clear and straightforward manner.

Each of the four sections on Energy, Electronics, Structures, and Mechanisms attempts to provide a balance of knowledge with understanding and application through the various practical activities. At the end of each section several design and technology problems are posed which use a working knowledge of appropriate concepts.

The material in this book formed part of curriculum development in Craft Design and Technology in the first three years of secondary education in the Cambridgeshire Education Authority. The original project was made possible with the help of a grant from the School Curriculum Development Committee.

I should like to thank my co-author, John Saxton, for developing parts of this work book, initiating others and trialling the practical activities during his period of secondment in the Cambridgeshire Authority: and the staff of the Science department at Homerton College for their support during this period.

In addition, I should like to express my appreciation to the Chief Education Officer, Mr. G. Morris and the Deputy Chief Officer, Mr. B. Oakley-Smith for their continued support and to the Wardens and Teachers of the many Village Colleges who supported the piloting of the activities which we have included.

Complete lists of components for the Electronics element are available from the Cambridgeshire LEA, Ely Resource Unit, telephone Ely 3486.

K.A. Shooter
Inspector for Design
and Technology
Cambridgeshire LEA
January 1987

Part 1 Energy

Harnessing energy

Homo sapiens is only one of a huge number and variety of different species which inhabit the Earth. Compared with many of the large species of animals, humans are physically quite weak. Yet humans dominate the Earth!

Today there are over four thousand million people living on Earth. They live in surroundings as different as the arctic ice and the tropical jungle. They have climbed the highest mountains and explored the ocean floor: some have even left the planet for a short time and visited the moon!

Why did this happen? What was it that enabled *Homo sapiens* to turn itself into the most successful of all species?

In fact, these dramatic developments are the result of humans using their intellect and manual skill to exploit the environment and to shape it to their needs. Discovering the Earth's reservoirs of **energy** and learning how to use them have enabled us to build the highly technological civilisation in which we live.

1 Energy: what is it?

Wherever and whenever any **work** is done, **energy** is needed to do it. For example, turning the pages of this book is work, and energy is needed to do it.

Energy is the **capacity for doing work**. You can think of energy as 'stored work'.

1.1 Forms of energy

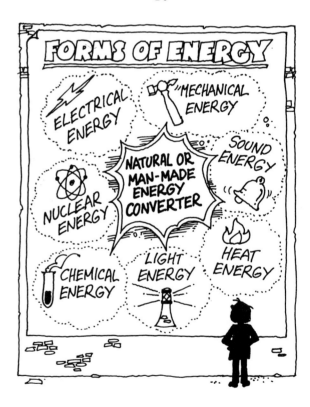

Energy can exist in a number of different forms and can change from one form to another. It often does this naturally (think of what happens in a thunderstorm, for example), but people have learned how to make it change form for their own benefit.

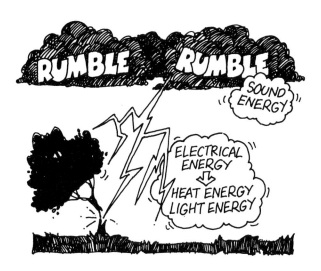

kinetic energy, whereas a brick falling from a chimney has a lot more kinetic energy. A lorry travelling at a fast speed has more kinetic energy that a similar lorry travelling at a slow speed.

How much kinetic energy a moving object has depends on its speed (or **velocity**) and its **mass** (the amount of 'matter' in it). You can measure how much kinetic energy an object has by the amount of work that would have to be done to stop the object moving.

1.2 Mechanical energy

Mechanical energy is one form of energy. It can be either potential or kinetic energy.

Potential energy is often called 'stored energy'. If we lift a book from the floor and put it on a table or a shelf, the work we have done has not been 'wasted'. It has been stored in the book as potential energy. This is because of the book's **position** – its height from the floor. If we wind up a clockwork toy, we are storing potential energy in its spring. Potential energy in this case is stored in the toy because of its **state** – the spring being wound up.

All moving objects have **kinetic energy**. A feather falling from a bird has a tiny amount of

Activity 1

In this activity you are going to make a model which demonstrates potential and kinetic energy. You need a paper clip, a soft drinks can, a large bead, an elastic band and a piece of cane or dowelling about 80 mm long.

Preparation of materials

Cane or dowelling
Measure 50 mm from one end and mark the stick with a pencil. Saw the stick into two pieces at this point.

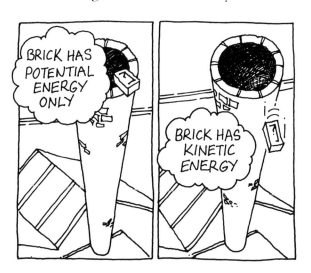

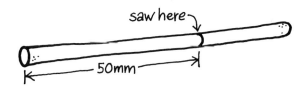

3

Paper clip

Straighten out this bend.

Put the 50 mm stick like this.

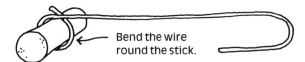

Bend the wire round the stick.

Thread the bead on the wire.

Soft drinks can

Drill a 5 mm diameter hole in the bottom of the soft drinks can.

How can I hold the can safely and securely while I drill it?

How do I find the centre of the can accurately?

Putting the parts together

Push the elastic band halfway into the can through the ring-pull hole. To stop the band from going completely into the can, put the short piece of cane or dowelling across the ring-pull hole, like this.

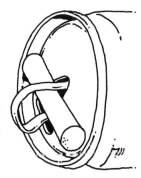

Use a hook, to pull the elastic band out through the other end of the can.

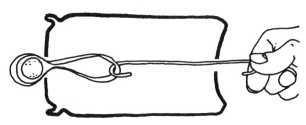

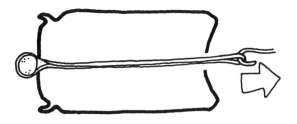

Attach the hook of the paper clip to the elastic band. Allow the elastic band to pull the paper clip into the can until the bead rests against the can.

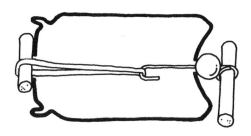

Using the model

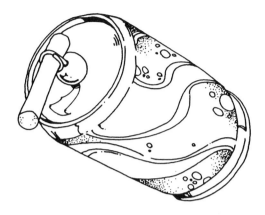

1 Give the model some potential energy by holding the can steady in one hand and turning the stick through 10 revolutions with the other. (You may need to increase or decrease the number of turns, depending on the thickness and length of the elastic band.)
Don't release the stick yet!

Potential energy (the capacity for doing work) has now been stored in your model. The work you did in turning the stick has not been wasted – quite a lot of it has been changed into potential energy stored in the elastic band. This is an example of energy changing form. The energy in your muscles has been changed into another form in the model: mechanical energy in the form of potential energy.

2 Put the can carefully on the floor, let it go and see what happens.

If nothing happens, try turning the stick a few more times. If the model still doesn't work, check that you made it correctly.

When you released the model, it did some work – it moved along the floor. The potential energy which you had put into the model was gradually released and changed into kinetic energy. The moving model has kinetic energy.

2 Making your model more efficient

Your drinks can machine is a simple working model which demonstrates the two types of mechanical energy: potential and kinetic energy. Your task now is to make your model work better by making it more efficient – so that it will travel the maximum distance across the floor for a given amount of energy. Doing this will introduce you to some of the ways scientists, technologists and engineers work.

There are three stages involved here.

To solve this problem you will have to work methodically rather than just guess!

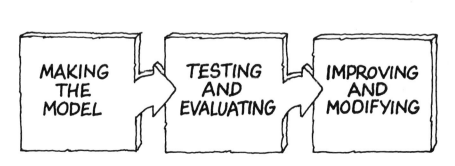

MAKING THE MODEL → TESTING AND EVALUATING → IMPROVING AND MODIFYING

2.1 Testing and evaluating

Activity 2

1 Mark a starting line.

2 Give your model some potential energy (about 10 turns of the stick, but this will depend on your elastic band).

3 Release your model from the starting line. Measure the distance it travels. Write it down.

4 You have now measured the distance travelled by your model when it was given a certain amount of energy. How far do you think it will travel if you do the test again? Write your prediction in a table like this.

Test number	Predicted distance	Actual distance
1		
2		
3		
4		
5		

5 Now test your prediction. Write your result in the table.

6 Do this four more times. Predict the distance the model will travel, then test your prediction. Make sure you give your model the same amount of potential energy each time.

You will have found that your model's performance was different on each test, even though you tried to give it the same amount of energy each time. This makes it difficult to make an accurate prediction of how far the model will travel on a test. What you can do instead is to give your prediction as a **range** or as an **average**, based on the results of your previous tests.

Range

The range is given by the shortest and longest distances travelled in the tests.

Example. Given 10 full turns of the stick, the model will travel a distance in the range of 4.95 m to 5.35 m.

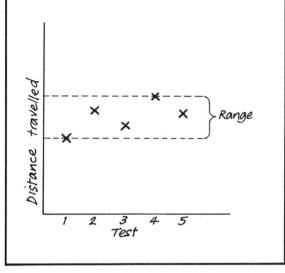

Average

The average is worked out by adding all the distances and then dividing by the number of tests.

Example. Given 10 full turns of the stick, the model will travel an average of 5.25 m.

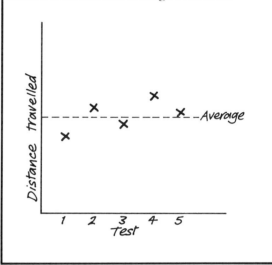

Activity 3

Try giving your test results as a range and as an average. You might like to draw a graph.

Trying something only once is not an accurate way of testing and evaluating your model. The more tests you make, record and analyse, the more accurate your evaluation of the model will be.

2.2 Modifying and improving

Now that you know what your model can do, you can try changing (modifying) it to make it more efficient. You will need to test the changes you make, to check that they work. Once again it is better to work methodically rather than by trial and error.

Activity 4

1 Think about your model.
   • Did it slip?
   • Did it make a noise?
   • Was there still some energy left when it came to rest?
And so on.

7

2   Make a table like this.

Modification number	Modification	Reasons for the modification	Numbers of tests done	Results- was the change an improvement?

Think about how you could solve the different problems. Write down the modifications you would like to make in the second column, and why you want to make them in the third column.

3   Now make the modifications and test them. (It is best to try one modification at a time. If you change more than one thing at a time, you won't be able to tell what is happening – one modification might be improving your model, but the other making it worse).

Optional work

1 Test your model with *x* turns of the stick. Record the results. You decide how big *x* is. It might be 3, 4, 5, 6, etc. turns depending on your elastic band. Choose a number which stores only a small amount of potential energy at first.

2 Test your model with 2*x* turns of the stick. Record the results. (If you chose *x* to be 3 turns, then 2*x* would be 2 × 3 = 6 turns, for example.)

3 Using the information from these tests, predict how far the model will travel when given 3*x* and 4*x* turns of the stick. Your predictions can be given as an average distance or a range of distances, or both.

4 Test your predictions for 3*x* and 4*x* turns of the stick. Record the results.

5 Explain the results.

3 Work and power

3.1 Work

We know that energy is the ability to do **work**. Mechanical energy is one form of energy, and can be either potential energy or kinetic energy. Potential energy is **work** stored in an object because of its position or state, or both. Kinetic energy is the energy which all moving objects have. The amount of kinetic energy a moving object has is the same as the amount of **work** that would have to be done to stop it.

A term that keeps cropping up here is **work**. So, what is work?

Work is being done whenever there is **movement against an opposing force**. Turning the pages of this book is doing work. Even though it might seem quite easy to do this work (turning the pages!), you still need to use energy to do it.

If you lift a book from the table, you are doing work. If you lift three books from the table, you are doing more work because you have to apply a bigger force. There is a formula which tells us how to find out how much work is done.

Amount of   =   Force   ×   Distance moved in the
work done   direction of force

Force is measured in **newtons (N)**. Distance is measured in **metres (m)**. Work is measured in **joules (J)**. In fact, 1 joule is the amount of work done when a force of 1 newton moves through a distance of 1 metre.

Suppose this miner uses a force of 20N to move the trolley 5m. We can find out the amount of work done like this:

Work done = Force × Distance moved
$$= 20 \times 5$$
$$= 100J$$

9

Activity 5

Calculate the work done by this gantry crane when it raises a load 8 metres, using a force of 50 N.

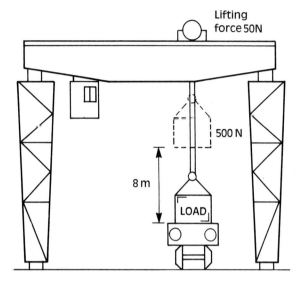

Activity 6

You can find out more about work by using a model crane like this. You can make the crane from scraps of wood, metal or plastic, or you can use a construction kit.

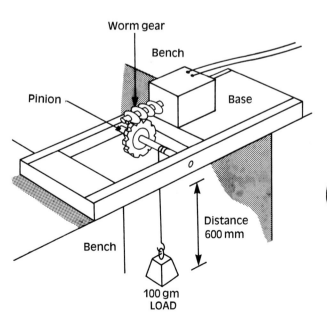

Here is an example of what you might do with your crane.

Suppose the model crane lifts a 100 gram mass through a distance of 600 mm. How much work has been done?

First you need to know the size of the opposing force. You can find this out by using a newton-meter to measure the weight of the mass.

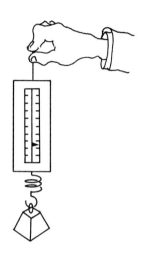

For a 100 gram mass, the force is about **1 newton**. The distance moved is 600 mm, or **0.6 m**. Now you can use the formula.

Work done = Force × Distance moved
= 1 N   × 0.6 m
= 0.6 J

So the crane did 0.6 joules of work in this case.

Try different masses and find out how much work your own crane can do.

When you've studied mechanisms, you may be able to make your crane work more efficiently

3.2 Power

A crane which does the same amount of work as another crane but in a shorter time is said to be more **powerful**. **Power** can be explained as the **rate of doing work**. The formula for working out power is

$$\text{Power} = \frac{\text{Work done}}{\text{Time taken}}$$

Power is measured in **watts (W)**. The work done is measured in joules (J). The time taken is measured in seconds (s).

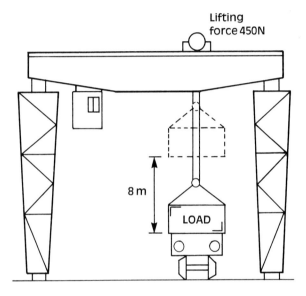

Lifting force 450N

8 m

LOAD

Suppose this gantry crane lifts a load 8 metres in 3 minutes, using a force of 450 N. How much power has been used?

Work done = Force X Distance moved
= 450 x 8
= 3600 J

Time taken = 3 minutes
= 180 seconds

Power = $\frac{\text{Work done}}{\text{Time taken}}$

$= \frac{3600}{180}$

$= 20\,W$

Activity 7

How powerful is the crane you made in activity 6? Find out by using a stopwatch to measure the time it takes to lift different masses the same distance. You will need to work with a friend. One of you uses the stopwatch and says when to start and stop the crane, and the other operates the crane's motor.

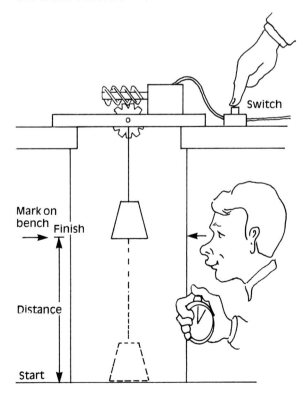

Switch

Mark on bench
Finish

Distance

Start

11

You might like to put your results in a table like this.

Load (N)	Distance (m)	Work done (J)	Time taken (s)	Power (W)

Energy word search

```
M X W A I T W S C O K S T Q E R T Y I O L F V G
A E A S D F O T R E W Q U I O P L K J H N M E B
S V C D W A R I N O P O T A N T I O M E T E L R
H S O H B I K T H A E(E N E R G Y)T S D F K O L
L M E P A W S A C X P O A J K H O P S F K L C M
N E P S D N K L M N E P R E W D S A C X I K I L
M O M C D A I S G T Y H D H J K L P O I M N T B
H P O T I U M C L K J R T E F C V I A M U J Y O
O C R E T Y U P A D I J K A E H O L M N A B V I
I O D F G E U M N L I G H T B E A T V B N S J T
A O P E I W T D A T E C H N I C A L V R T H S D
H E P I F H K C L O E I D R I W A F T V C E N R
T W U R A R I A S N A I O M N I A R S T A U K E
R E S N I R I O P R E S E T O N S E T P O W E R
D A R O T M T H J E R H M I S T O R E S G I M E
N T P C O R T A O F C A L L Y I N G V O L T N A
I U E A G I O L U D S R S V I L K D F I A R L T
W L E R S N U C L E A R V I S T O R S P I A N K
E P C I O T R E E A N M R I O T K S U K I Q U N
O D F H M E A K S T U D B I K E U I L T C K A S
I O R R E M T G T Z I O T L I K E P N R A K I O
R P S O U N D M C T S E W A E R I E M E N O R R
S P R E E P I R I O M S S V F S T W I O T D W P
H K L M O E O C E R S E I T E O R F A C E I S I
N E W T O N S U A M S T O L P I S M O U T E C R
```

Find the following words, which have been used in this part of the book. ENERGY is done for you

MECHANICAL	HEAT	SOUND
WORK	MASS	NEWTONS
ELECTRICAL	LIGHT	POTENTIAL
VELOCITY	POWER	JOULES
NUCLEAR	CHEMICAL	KINETIC

Don't write on the book! Ask your teacher for a copy of this page.

Part 2 Electronics

Electricity, scientists and technologists

If you were to ask people when they thought electricity was first discovered, many of them would probably say that it wasn't very long ago – within the last hundred years or so.

They would be completely wrong! People have known about electricity for more than 2000 years! The ancient Greeks knew that if you rub amber with a piece of fur it will attract light objects like small pieces of paper. They used the words ελεκτροσ to describe this phenomenon. Our word **electricity** is derived from this.

However, it is true that electricity has been put to use only in the last hundred years or so. During this period, scientists made a number of important discoveries about electricity, and presented this new knowledge to society. Engineers then applied this knowledge to create devices and machines which perform physical work, provide light and heat, and enable communication over enormous distances at incredible speed.

Engineers and technologists have an enormous responsibility. Although scientists discover the knowledge initially, technologists **translate** the knowledge into useful devices and machines. The work of technologists **affects** our society, and so technologists need to consider the social, moral and ethical consequences of the solutions they provide to the different problems.

1 Electricity: what is it?

Electrical energy is a very useful form of energy. It can be easily changed to many other forms of energy to do useful work. This picture shows electrical energy being changed into other forms. What kinds can you see? What carries the electrical energy to the different things?

Electricity flows through the wires to the different things. The electric current is made up of tiny moving particles called **electrons**. Electronics puts these moving electrons to work in a useful way.

1.1 Electronic circuits

Electronic circuits are made from parts called **components**. Usually these components are soldered into circuits, as you can see from this photo of the inside of a personal stereo. Some of the components here are integrated circuits (ICs) and others are discrete (separate) components.

Activity 1

You will be making circuits from discrete components only, using a 'dry construction' technique instead of soldering. In the first circuit, you will make a lamp light up.

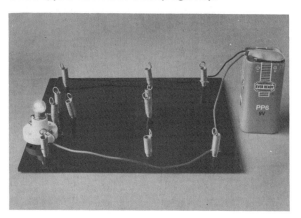

Materials needed

A baseboard, a 9 volt battery, a few lengths of red wire, a few lengths of black wire, a lamp-holder and bulb, and a pair of long-nosed pliers. Details of the circuit baseboard can be found on page 85.

Making the circuit

1 This plan shows how the components should be connected, using the springs on the baseboard. ⟨ ⟩ shows springs that are not used in this circuit.

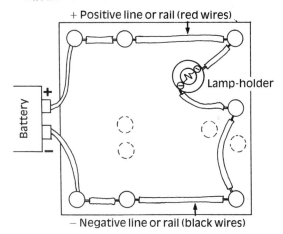

+ Positive line or rail (red wires)

Lamp-holder

Battery

– Negative line or rail (black wires)

2 Make the circuit, but **do not connect the battery yet!** Lift the connecting springs carefully using long-nosed pliers.

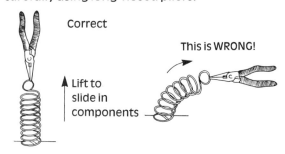

Correct

This is WRONG!

Lift to slide in components

Slide in the leads of the component, then release the spring. Additional components joining the spring will fit in at different levels.

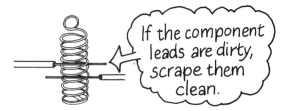

If the component leads are dirty, scrape them clean.

3 Check that you have made the circuit correctly.

4 Now connect the battery. Connect the red wires (+) first and the black wires (−) second. What happens?

5 Disconnect the battery. What happens?

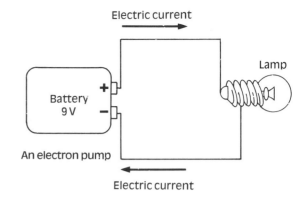

Electric current

Lamp

Battery
9 V

+

−

An electron pump

Electric current

ALWAYS
Check the circuit carefully BEFORE you connect the battery.
ALWAYS
disconnect the battery BEFORE you alter the circuit or take it to bits.

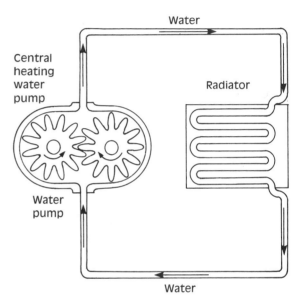

Water

Central heating water pump

Radiator

Water pump

Water

When the battery is connected, electricity flows through the circuit and the lamp lights up. You can think of the battery as a pump, pushing the electric current through the circuit rather like a central-heating pump pushes water through the pipes and radiators.

Conventionally, the electric current flows out of the positive terminal of the battery, down the positive line (the red wires), through the lamp, and then to the negative terminal of the battery through the negative line (the black wires). We always draw electric currents as flowing from positive to negative.

In fact, scientists have found that in an electric current the flow of electrons is from negative to positive. Unfortunately, when batteries were invented and electric currents first investigated, although scientists knew something was moving, they wrongly guessed that it was moving from positive to negative. We have, for some strange reason, kept with this convention when drawing circuit diagrams, but you should remember that the electrons are really moving in the opposite direction to 'conventional current'.

Diagrams for electronic circuits use special symbols. For example, the diagram for the circuit you have made looks like this.

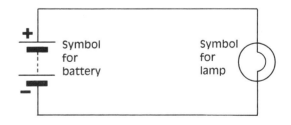

+

Symbol for battery

Symbol for lamp

−

1.2 Controlling the circuit

If you connect and disconnect the battery, you can **control** the circuit – you can turn the lamp

15

on and off. You can also control the circuit by 'breaking' (or **opening**) it. Try this.

Activity 2

1 Make the circuit as in activity 1. Keep the battery connected.

2 Disconnect one end of the red wire (the positive line). What happens to the lamp? Is current flowing through the circuit now?

3 Put the end of the wire against the spring from which it was removed. What happens?

Electric current will only flow in a **closed** circuit. If there are any breaks in the circuit (if the circuit is **open**), the current will not flow.

One way of controlling whether or not current flows through a circuit is to use a **switch**. When the switch is 'off', the circuit is open and no current flows.

Two common switches are the rocker switch and the dry reed switch.

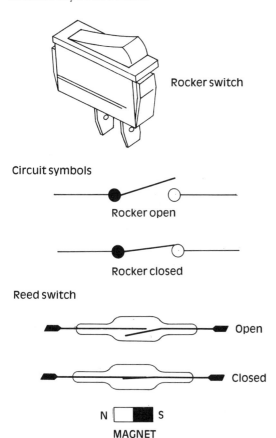

Rocker switch

Circuit symbols

Rocker open

Rocker closed

Reed switch

Open

Closed

N ☐ S
MAGNET

The reed switch consists of two steel contacts in a small glass case filled with nitrogen. A reed switch is normally open, until you hold a magnet near to it. Then the contacts will be attracted to each other and the circuit closed. If you use two magnets as in the diagram below, you can change the way the switch works. Try it out in activity 3.

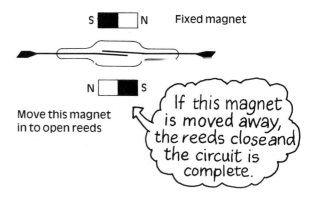

S ☐ N   Fixed magnet

N ☐ S

Move this magnet in to open reeds

If this magnet is moved away, the reeds close and the circuit is complete.

Activity 3

1 Modify your circuit by fitting a rocker switch.

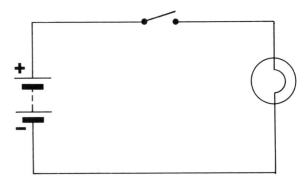

2 Replace the rocker switch with a reed switch. Use just one magnet. How can you turn the lamp on and off now?

3 Experiment with the reed switch and two magnets. What do you have to do now to turn the lamp on and off?

Design technology project

Design and make a simple alarm system which can be used to prevent an object from being moved from where it is. The system will have two parts.

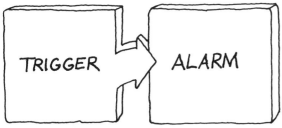

The trigger for the alarm can be placed on top of or beneath the object – a book or box. The trigger will be some kind of switch which **closes** the circuit if the object is moved.

The alarm can be raised by a lamp or a buzzer.

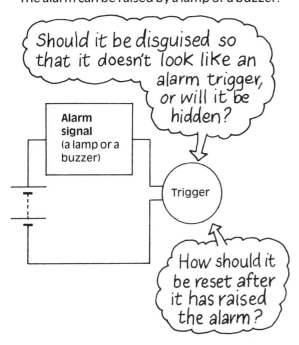

Optional work

Find out about the different alarm systems used in shops and libraries. What are the triggers like? What kinds of alarm signals are used?

2 Looking at circuits

2.1 Measuring potential differences

In the circuit you have just made, the battery supplied electrical energy which was turned into heat and light energy by the filament of the lamp. The battery is an electron pump which pushes electrons around a circuit. The electrical pressure in the battery which does this is called the **e.m.f.** (electro-motive force). The e.m.f. is measured in units called **volts (V)**. The battery you used in the lamp circuit has an e.m.f. of 9 volts – in other words, it pumps electrons around the circuit with an electrical pressure of 9 volts.

Your next task is to look at the electrical pressure difference – called the **potential difference** or **'voltage'** – at different places in your circuit, using a **voltmeter**.

A voltmeter measures voltage. Its scale shows volts (V) or millivolts ($1000\,\text{mV} = 1\,\text{V}$). To measure the potential difference across a component, the voltmeter needs to be connected in parallel with (alongside) the component. The voltmeter's positive (+) terminal should be connected to the higher voltage side (the side nearest the positive terminal of the battery), and the negative (−) terminal to the lower voltage side.

17

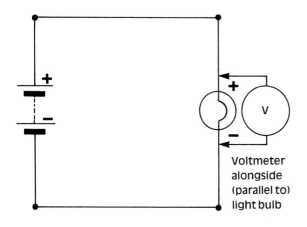

Voltmeter
alongside
(parallel to)
light bulb

Activity 4

1   Connect the voltmeter onto the circuit at V1.
Write down the reading.

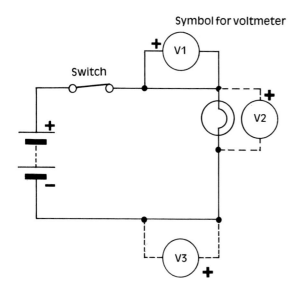

Symbol for voltmeter

2   Now connect the voltmeter at V2, and then at
V3. Write down the reading each time.

You should have found that the voltmeter
read '0V' at V1 and at V3. This is because these
readings were taken along electron-conducting
wire so there was almost no loss or drop in the
electrical pressure. In other words, there was
no potential difference. At V2 you got a reading
because across the lamp there was an electrical
pressure difference – a potential difference.

2.2 Series and parallel circuits

'In series' means 'one after the other'. In the
circuit below, the two lamps are in series with
each other.

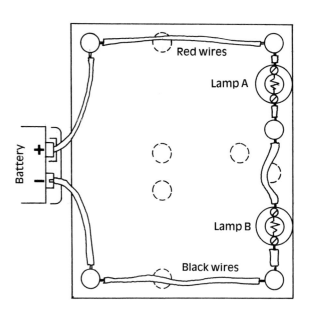

Activity 5

1   (a) Redraw the above circuit diagram, but use
circuit symbols.
     (b) Construct the circuit.
Use the circuit to find out the answers to these
questions.

2   Are the lamps brighter, dimmer or the same
as the lamp in activity 4?

3   What happens if bulb A is removed from its
holder? Why does this happen? (Put the bulb
back afterwards!)

4   Use the voltmeter to measure the potential
difference across bulb A.

5   Use the voltmeter to measure the potential
difference across bulb B.

6   Now use the voltmeter to measure the
potential difference across the battery.

7   Write down what you notice about the
readings you took in steps 4, 5 and 6.

'In parallel' means 'alongside'. In the next
circuit, the two lamps are parallel to each other.

18

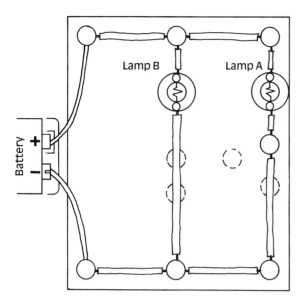

show amperes (A) or milliamperes (1000 mA = 1 A). To measure the current at a point in the circuit, the circuit needs to be broken at that point and the ammeter connected in series. The ammeter's positive terminal should be connected to the higher voltage side, and the negative terminal to the lower voltage side.

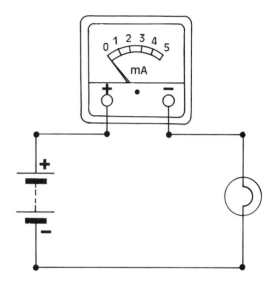

Activity 6

1 (a) Redraw the above circuit diagram, but use circuit symbols.
(b) Construct the circuit.
Use the circuit to find out the answers to these questions.

2 Are the bulbs brighter, dimmer or the same as they were in activity 4?

3 What happens if you remove bulb A from its holder? Why do you think this happens?

4 What happens if you remove bulb B from its holder? Why?

5 Use the voltmeter to measure the potential difference across bulb A, then across bulb B and finally across the battery. Write down what you notice.

2.3 Measuring electric currents

The number of electrons which flow in a given time is a measure of the quantity of electricity flowing in a circuit. The quantity of electricity flowing is called the **current** and is measured in units called **amperes** (often shortened to **amps**).

In the next activity you are going to use an ammeter to find out what happens to the current in a circuit.

An **ammeter** measures current. Its scales

Activity 7

1 Use the circuit you made in activity 6, with two lamps in parallel. Connect the ammeter in series into the circuit at A1. Write down its reading.

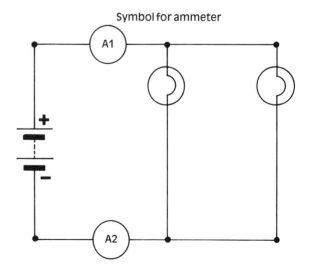

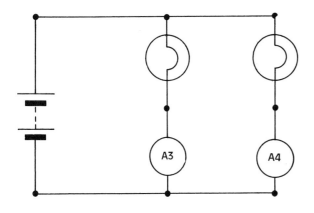

2 Now connect the ammeter at A2. Write down its reading.

3 What do you notice about the readings at A1 and A2?

4 Connect the ammeter at A3 and then at A4. Write down its reading each time.

5 What do you notice about the readings at A3 and A4?

6 Now compare readings A1 and A2 with readings A3 and A4. Write down what you notice.

3 Resistance and resistors

3.1 Resistors

All components and wires **resist** the flow of electric current, although some resist it more than others. The amount of **resistance** a component has is measured in **ohms** (symbol Ω). Big resistances can be measured in kilohms ($1\,k\Omega = 1000\,\Omega$) or even megohms ($1\,M\Omega = 1\,000\,000\,\Omega$).

We can control the amount of current flowing in a circuit by using **resistors**, which have a measured amount of resistance.

Resistors control the amount of current flowing in a circuit rather like people standing on a hosepipe control the amount of water flowing through it!

Resistors have four coloured bands. The first three say how much resistance the resistor has. The fourth band gives the tolerance (usually 5% or 10%). This table shows the resistor colour code.

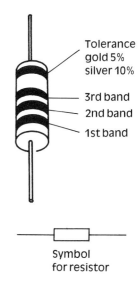

Tolerance
gold 5%
silver 10%

3rd band
2nd band
1st band

Symbol
for resistor

1st band 1st digit		2nd band 2nd digit		3rd band Number of zeros	
Black	0	Black	0	Black	0 zero –
Brown	1	Brown	1	Brown	1 zero – 0
Red	2	Red	2	Red	2 zeros – 00
Orange	3	Orange	3	Orange	3 zeros – 000
Yellow	4	Yelow	4	Yelow	4 zeros – 0000
Green	5	Green	5	Green	5 zeros – 00000
Blue	6	Blue	6	Blue	6 zeros – 000000
Violet	7	Violet	7	Silver	× 0.01
Grey	8	Grey	8	Gold	× 0.1
White	9	White	9		

Here are some examples to show you how the code works.

1st band		2nd band		3rd band		Value of resistor
Yellow	4	Violet	7	Red	00	$4700\,\Omega = 4.7\,k\Omega$
Brown	1	Black	0	Green	00000	$1\,000\,000\,\Omega = 1\,M\Omega$
Blue	6	Grey	8	Gold	x0.1	$68 \times 0.1\,\Omega = 6.8\,\Omega$

Optional work

Draw and colour resistors of the following values. Colour the fourth band silver (for tolerance = 10%).

4.7Ω, 56Ω, 100Ω, 330Ω, 1kΩ, 18kΩ.

Note. Only certain preferred resistor values are manufactured. These are:

1, 1.2, 1.5, 1.8, 2.2, 2.7, 3.3, 3.9, 4.7, 5.6, 6.8, 8.2

and multiples of these by

10, 100, 1000, 10000, 100000, 1000000.

This means that you may have to approximate and use the nearest available value when you are designing a circuit.

Activity 8

In this activity you will find out what happens when you put different amounts of resistance into the simple lamp circuit.

1 Find these four resistors: 47 Ω, 100 Ω, 330 Ω, 1 kΩ. (You can use the resistor colour code table to check that you have the right values.)

2 Construct this circuit. First use the 47 Ω resistor at X, then the 100 Ω, then the 330 Ω, and finally the 1 kΩ.

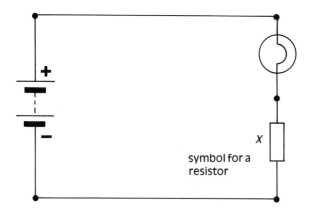

symbol for a resistor

3 Write down what happens to the brightness of the bulb as you use the different resistors. Which resistor seems to turn the lamp off? Is there current flowing when this happens? (How could you check for this?)

4 Repeat stage 2 of this activity, but this time use a voltmeter to check the potential differences across the lamp and each resistor. (Take readings at V1 and V2.)

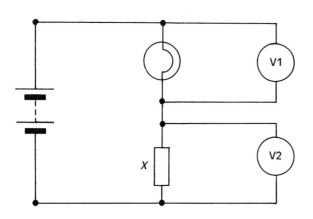

You might like to write your readings in a table like this.

What do you notice?

Activity 9

1 Use a 470 Ω variable resistor (potentiometer) instead of a fixed resistor at X. Turn the spindle of the potentiometer slowly. Write down what happens to the lamp as you turn the spindle clockwise and then anticlockwise.

Potentiometer or variable resistor

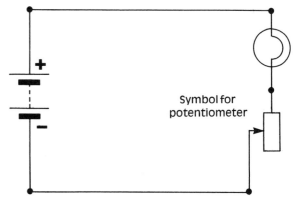

Symbol for potentiometer

2 Now replace the lampholder with a small electric motor (6 or 9V). Write down what happens when you turn the spindle of the potentiometer.

Design technology project

Electric food mixers can usually work at three speeds – slow, medium or fast. The person using the mixer chooses the speed he or she wants.

Your task is to design and build a circuit which allows someone to control how fast the mixer goes. (Use a small electric motor to represent the mixer.)

3.2 Ohm's law

In electronics, letters are often used to stand for the values of current, potential difference and resistance. The letters used are:

I for current in amperes, for example $I = 0.06A$

V for potential difference in volts, for example $V = 4.5V$

These Vs mean different things. Don't get confused! V stands for potential difference while V is the symbol for volts.

R for resistance in ohms, for example $R = 4.7\,\Omega$

Activity 10

1 Construct this circuit. (You can choose which values of resistors to use for R1, R2 and R3.)

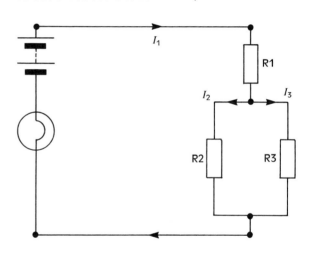

Make a table like this, and write down your resistor values in the column labelled *R*.

Resistor	R	I	V
R1	$R_1 =$ Ω	$I_1 =$ A	$V_1 =$ V
R2	$R_2 =$ Ω	$I_2 =$ A	$V_2 =$ V
R3	$R_3 =$ Ω	$I_3 =$ A	$V_3 =$ V

2 Use an ammeter to measure the current through R1, R2 and then R3. Write your results in the table, in the column labelled I.

3 Use a voltmeter to measure the potential difference across R1, R2 and then R3. Write your results in the table.

4 Look at your results. Try adding I_2 and I_3, and compare the result with I_1. What do you notice? Compare V_2 and V_3. Should you be surprised?

You should have found that the current flowing through a component is affected by both its resistance and the potential difference across it. In fact, current, potential difference and resistance are linked by **Ohm's law**.

Optional work

Look at the table you made in activity 10. Use a calculator to work out $I \times R$ for each resistor. (First make sure that the values of I are in amps, not milliamps.) Are the results what you would expect?

3.3 Using Ohm's law to check the value of resistors

Ohm's law says that if a conductor has a resistance of R ohms and a potential difference of V volts across it, and the current flowing through it is I amps, then

$$V = I \times R \quad \text{or} \quad I = \frac{V}{R} \quad \text{or} \quad R = \frac{V}{I}.$$

These formulas are used a lot in electronics. You might find it easier to remember them if you think of this symbol:

Activity 11

How accurate are resistors? Do they really have the resistance their coloured bands say they have? You can use the circuit shown below to check them.

1 Set up the circuit. Find some resistors to check, for example 33 Ω, 47 Ω, 56 Ω, 68 Ω and 100 Ω. Connect each resistor between the crocodile clips and make a note of the voltmeter and ammeter readings (you might like to do this in a table, as in activity 10).

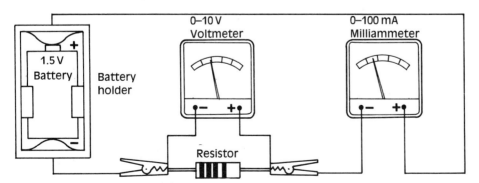

2 Now you can use Ohm's law $R = \frac{V}{I}$ to work out the 'real' resistance of each resistor.

For example, if you were using a 47 Ω resistor and got I = 30 mA and V = 1.45 V, Ohm's law would give

$$R = \frac{V}{I} = \frac{1.45}{0.03} = 48.33$$

So the 'real' resistance of this 47 Ω resistor is 48.33 Ω!

3   Did you find that the 'real' resistance of your resistors was different from what the coloured bands said? Even so, your resistors might not be marked wrongly. You need to look at the fourth band – the **tolerance** – to check this. If this band is silver (10% tolerance) and the marked resistance is R, the resistor's real resistance should lie between

$R - (10\%$ of $R)$ and $R + (10\%$ of $R)$

So a 47 Ω resistor with a silver tolerance band should have a resistance of between

47 − (10% of 47) = 47 − 4.7 = 42.3 Ω

and

47 + (10% of 47) = 47 + 4.7 = 51.7 Ω

A gold tolerance band shows a tolerance of 5%. Check that your resistors have resistances within their tolerance range.

3.4 Resistors in series and in parallel

Resistors are often combined to obtain different resistances. In this section we shall look at the total resistance of resistors connected in series and then in parallel.

When resistors are connected **in series**, their total resistance R_s is found by adding the individual resistances.

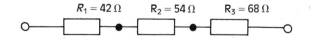

$R_1 = 42\ \Omega$ $R_2 = 54\ \Omega$ $R_3 = 68\ \Omega$

$$\begin{aligned}\text{Total resistance} &= R_1 + R_2 + R_3 \\ &= 42 + 54 + 68 \\ &= 164\ \Omega\end{aligned}$$

When resistors are connected **in parallel** their total resistance R_p is found by using this formula:

$$\frac{1}{R_p} = \frac{1}{R_1} + \frac{1}{R_2} + \frac{1}{R_3} + \ldots$$

For example, for these resistors connected in parallel,

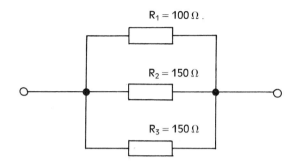

$R_1 = 100\ \Omega$

$R_2 = 150\ \Omega$

$R_3 = 150\ \Omega$

their total resistance is found like this:

$$\begin{aligned}\frac{1}{R_p} &= \frac{1}{100} + \frac{1}{150} + \frac{1}{150} \\ &= 0.01 + 0.006\,66\ldots + 0.006\,66\ldots \\ &= 0.023\,33\ldots\end{aligned}$$

Use a calculator to work these out!

$$\text{So } R_p = \frac{1}{0.023\,33\ldots} = 42.9\ \Omega$$

Notice that the total resistance of resistors in parallel is less than their individual resistances.

Activity 12

Try working out the total resistances of these.
1   Three resistors – 47 Ω, 330 Ω, 560 Ω – in series.

2   Two resistors – 270 Ω, 1.2 Ω – in series.

3   Three resistors – 100 Ω, 120 Ω, 150 Ω – in parallel.

4   Three resistors – 10 Ω, 150 Ω, 1 kΩ – in parallel.

4 Using transistors

4.1 Introducing transistors

The circuits you have made so far have not been very sensitive. All the components you have used are called **passive** electronic components; that is, they do not produce or amplify voltage, current or power.

In this section we will look at an **active** component, the transistor. A transistor can be used as a current amplifier and as a switch. You will find that a transistor acts as an amplifier by using a small input current to cause a large output current to flow in a circuit.

A transistor is a **semi-conductor** device. Its resistance can vary between the very low resistance of conductors (wires, for instance) and the extremely high resistance of insulators.

There are many types of transistor. Each is designed to do a different job. You are going to use a BFY51 or a 2N3053 in your circuits. These are **n–p–n transistors**.

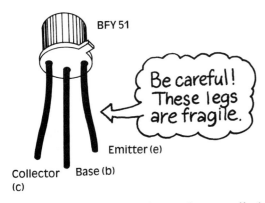

Be careful! These legs are fragile.

BFY 51

Emitter (e)

Collector (c)   Base (b)

Transistors have three legs, called the **collector** (c), the **base** (b) and the **emitter** (e). To work out which leg is which, compare your transistor with this underside view. Notice the tab which is used as a reference point.

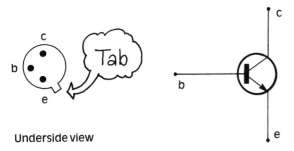

Tab

Underside view

In this transistor, conventional current flows **into the collector** and **out of the emitter**. (The arrow on the circuit symbol will help you to remember this.) In fact, current will only flow from c to e if a small control current flows into the base b. You will learn more about this in the next activity.

4.2 Using the transistor as a switch

Activity 13

1 Make this circuit.

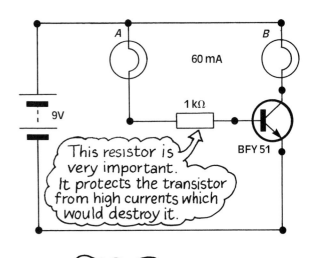

This resistor is very important. It protects the transistor from high currents which would destroy it.

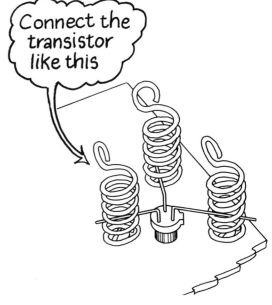

Connect the transistor like this

You should find that lamp *B* is on but lamp *A* is off. This shows that the current passing through *B* to the collector is greater than the current through *A* to the base connection of the transistor.

Unscrew lamp *A*. What happens?

This shows that the collector current will only flow when there is some current flowing through the base.

2 Change your circuit like this.

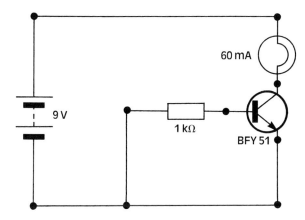

When you connect the battery, the lamp should remain off. Since there is no current at the transistor's base (remember that current flows from + to −), the collector–emitter resistance is **high**, the current at the collector is low and the lamp does not glow.

3 Change your circuit like this.

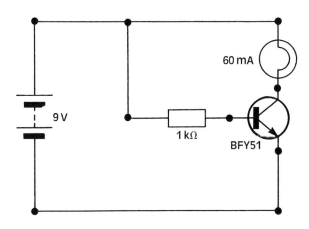

Connect the battery and watch what happens. Then copy and complete this sentence.

> When a small current is flowing into the base of the transistor, the collector-emitter resistance is ____, causing the lamp to glow.

Activity 14

If we want to use the transistor effectively as a switch, we need to **control the base current.**
1 Make this circuit.

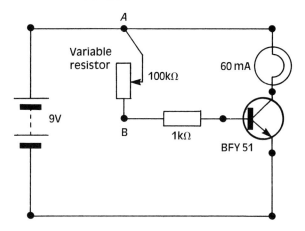

2 Turn the spindle of the variable resistor to increase its resistance. This will reduce the current flowing into the base of the transistor. Write down what this does to the resistance between the collector and emitter. Does it increase or decrease? What happens to the lamp?

3 Try to adjust the brightness of the lamp rather than just switch it on and off.

4.3 Making the transistor switch more sensitive

Although the circuits in activities 13 and 14 can be used to control the transistor, they are not very effective in reality. A better way is to control the voltage at the base of the transistor, using a **potential divider**. This makes the transistor circuit more sensitive.

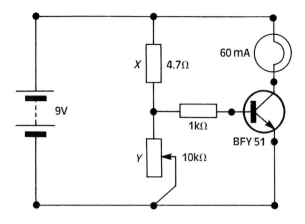

In this circuit, the potential divider uses two resistors at X and Y. These divide the supply voltage into two parts. The variable resistor at Y can be adjusted so that there is just enough current flowing into the base of the transistor to switch it on. In the circuit shown here, the BFY51 is switched on by a voltage of just over 0.6 V between the base and emitter.

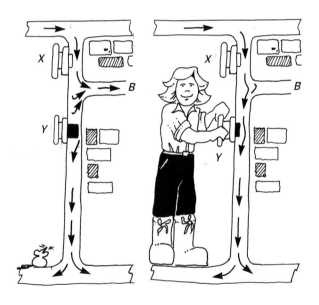

You can think of the potential divider as working like two valves in a water system. If valve Y is almost closed and valve X almost open, some water will flow into pipe B. However, if valve Y is almost open, the water will tend to bypass pipe B. In the potential divider, if variable resistor Y is set to a high resistance, the voltage at the base of the

transistor will be high, and so current will flow into the base, switching the transistor on. But if the variable resistor is set to a low resistance, the voltage at the transistor's base will be low, current will not flow into the base and the transistor will stay switched off.

Activity 15

Make the circuit shown opposite, using a 4.7 Ω resistor at X and a 10 kΩ variable resistor at Y. Adjust the variable resistor so that the transistor is just switched on (so the lamp just begins to glow). Then measure the voltage across the 1 kΩ resistor, using a voltmeter.

4.4 Using the transistor switch

The transistor switch can be used in many different circuits to do useful things. In this section you will use it to make a light-controlled switch, a heat-sensing device and a rain sensor. Before you do this, you need to know about two more semi-conductor devices – the **light-dependent resistor (LDR)** and the **thermistor**.

Light-dependent resistors are made from cadmium sulphide. Their resistance varies according to the amount of light they receive. In the dark a LDR has a high resistance, and in the light it has a low resistance.

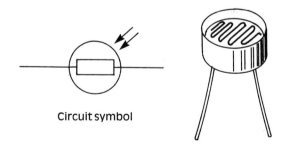

Circuit symbol

A thermistor – sometimes called a temperature-dependent resistor (TDR) – is sensitive to large temperature changes. The thermistor you will use is called an ntc rod thermistor (ntc stands for 'negative temperature coefficient'). As the temperature around an ntc thermistor increases, its resistance decreases.

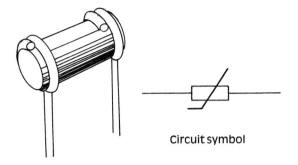

Circuit symbol

Activity 16

In this activity you will use the LDR ORP 12 to make a light-controlled switch.

Make a paper shield to increase the LDR's sensitivity.

BE CAREFUL! These legs are fragile. You might need to lengthen them by soldering on some extra wires

1 Make this circuit. Like other resistors, it does not matter which way round the LDR is connected.

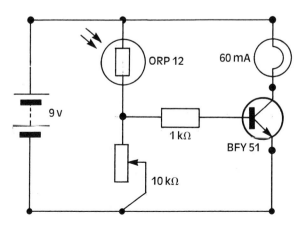

2 When the battery is connected, the lamp should glow if the room is well-lit. What happens to the lamp if you put your hand over the LDR? Write down your observations.

3 Reverse the positions of the LDR and the variable resistor. Write down what happens to the lamp when you put your hand over the LDR.

4 Try to think of some practical ways these circuits can be used.

Activity 17

In this activity you will make a heat-sensing circuit using the ntc rod thermistor TH3.

1 Make this circuit. Write down what happens to the lamp when you connect the battery.

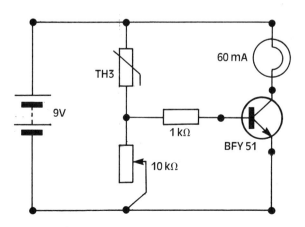

2 Hold a lighted match **carefully** under the thermistor. Write down what happens to the lamp.

3 Try to think how a circuit like this might be used.

In this circuit, at normal room temperatures of 20–25 °C, the thermistor has a high resistance of about 380 Ω. This means that the current flowing to the base of the transistor will be too low to switch the transistor on. The lamp in this case will not glow. When the thermistor is heated by the lighted match, its resistance decreases to below 30 Ω. This will allow enough current to flow to the base of the transistor to switch on the light.

Activity 18

You can make a rain sensor if you replace the thermistor in the circuit of activity 16 with a home-made rain-sensing device. When a drop of water or rain falls across any two strips of the device, the lamp will glow.

Materials needed

- A 20 × 20 mm piece of stripboard, hole pitch 0.1, hole diameter 1.0
- five pieces of 22 gauge insulated wire
- wire strippers
- solder and soldering iron

Making the device

1 Strip about 10 mm of insulation off each end of the wires. Twist the strands together.

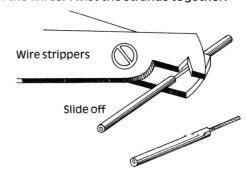

Wire strippers

Slide off

2 Coat the strands of wire with cored soft solder.

Soldering iron

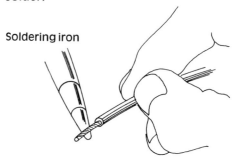

3 Solder the ends of the wires to the stripboard. The diagram shows where the wires should go.

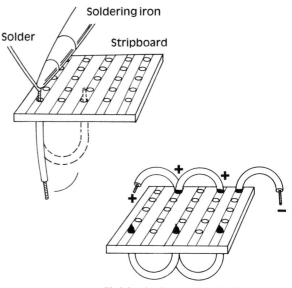

Soldering iron

Solder

Stripboard

Finished rain-sensing device

Design technology project

We want to time as accurately as possible how long a trolley takes to pass between two points as it rolls down a slope. We need some sort of signalling system; a signal when the trolley reaches the start position on the slope (so that we know when to start the stopwatch), and another signal to show when it reaches the finish position. These signals can be light or sound signals, or a combination of both. The start and the finish signals can be designed separately.

5 Capacitors and diodes

5.1 Time delay circuits

All the circuits you have made so far start working as soon as you connect the battery or switch them on. However, sometimes there needs to be a delay between the circuit being switched on and then working. For example, think about a circuit that switches on a street lamp when it gets dark. If there were no delay between the circuit detecting darkness and switching on the lamp, the lamp might be switched on every time a cloud obscured the sun for a few minutes.

Time delays can be built into circuits by using components called **capacitors**. Capacitors work by storing electricity.

Electrolytic capacitor

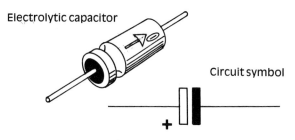

Circuit symbol

To understand how a capacitor works, look at the seesaw device below. The pin will burst the balloon only when enough water has been poured into the container. In the same way, the capacitor will only transfer voltage when it has been fully **charged**.

The ability of the capacitor to store electricity is called its **capacitance**. The larger the capacitance of a capacitor, the more electricity it can store. Different time delays can be built into circuits by using capacitors of different capacitances.

Capacitances are measured in **farads** (F) and **microfarads** (μF).

1 farad = 1 000 000 microfarads

The capacitors you will be using in your circuits are **electrolytic** capacitors. Their capacitances are usually measured in microfarads.

Two words of warning! Firstly, electrolytic capacitors can only withstand voltages up to the value printed on their case. Secondly, they must be connected the right way round. The positive end (shown by a 'necking in' on the case) must be connected to the positive side of the circuit.

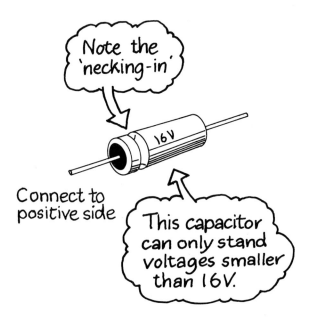

Activity 19

In this activity you are going to time the delays different capacitors can cause in a circuit. You will need a stopwatch to do this.

1 Make this circuit, using a 100 kΩ resistor and a 100 μF capacitor as shown. Do not connect the battery yet!

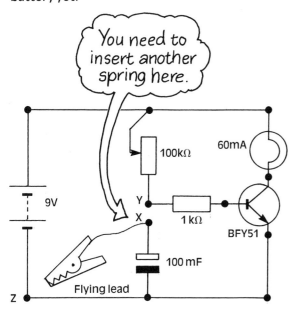

You need to insert another spring here.

100kΩ

60mA

9V

Y

X

1 kΩ

BFY51

100 mF

Flying lead

Z

2 Make sure that the capacitor is discharged. To do this, touch spring *Z* with the flying lead. Then attach the flying lead to spring *Y*, connect the battery and start the stopwatch. Stop the stopwatch as soon as the lamp lights. Write down the time delay for the 100 μF capacitor.

Although a capacitor is able to store an electric charge, there is a lot of difference between the energy stored in a large value capacitor and even the smallest battery. You would need a great many large value capacitors to store even the energy which is available in a small 1.5v torch battery

3 Disconnect the battery and replace the 100 μF capacitor with a 4700 μF capacitor. Discharge this new capacitor, then measure its time delay as before.

4 What do you notice about the time delays for the different capacitors?

Optional work

1 Instead of using a flying lead, you can use a single pole two-way switch.

2 If you adjust the 100 kΩ variable resistor, you can change the amount of delay produced. Try it out!

5.2 Protecting components

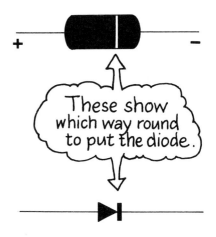

+   −

These show which way round to put the diode.

Diodes are components that allow current to flow in one direction only, rather like the valves in your veins keep your blood going the right way. They are used to protect other components in circuits. For example, transistors can be damaged by back voltages (electrons trying to go the wrong way), so diodes are used to protect them.

Not a lot of people know that!

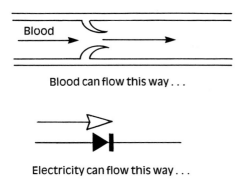

Blood can flow this way . . .

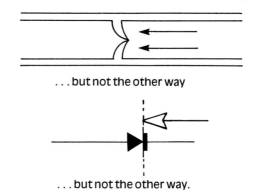

. . . but not the other way

Electricity can flow this way . . .

. . . but not the other way.

Diodes act like a valve in a vein.

Activity 20

1 Make this circuit. Write down what happens.

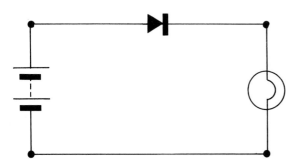

2 Turn the diode round. Write down what happens now.

3 Move the diode to the other side of the lamp, like this. Does this make any difference to how the diode works? Turn the diode round. What happens?

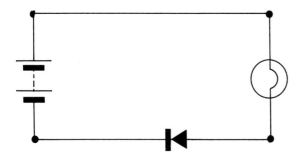

Activity 21

1 Make this circuit.

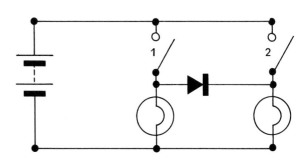

2 Close switch 1 and note down what happens.

3 Now open switch 1 and close switch 2. What happens?

4 Turn the diode round. Repeat steps 2 and 3. Write down what you notice about how the diode works.

Design technology projects

Use your knowledge of electronics to design and make a solution to one of these problems.

1 Design and make a circuit that will turn a lamp on when darkness falls. The lamp should not be switched on when there is a sudden but short time of darkness – so, for example, if the LDR is covered by a shadow for a few seconds the lamp should remain off.

A six hour delay does seem a bit long.

2 Design and make a temperature-controlled heating device for a small tank used for growing delicate plants or keeping a small snake. The tank is a small fish aquarium, $12\,000\,cm^3$ in volume. For both plants and snakes, it is important that the temperature inside the tank should not drop below a certain point (find out what this is for most delicate plants, and what it is for small snakes). If this point is reached, a heater – a lamp – should be switched on. When the temperature has risen to an acceptable level, the heater should be switched off.

3 Design and make a device to be attached to the front of a car that will warn the driver of ice. When the air temperature drops to about freezing point and ice is liable to be formed on the road, the device should give an audible or visible warning to the driver.

Never knew you did stunt driving, Mum!

4 You are the proud owner of a small but leaky cabin cruiser. Every now and then you have to pump out the water at the bottom of the boat – otherwise the boat will sink! Design and make a device that warns when the water level in the boat is getting too high, so that you can switch on the pump in time.

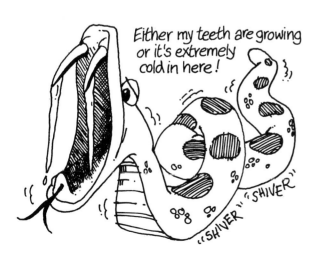

Either my teeth are growing or it's extremely cold in here!

"SHIVER" "SHIVER"

BUZZ BUZZ

There it goes! Time to start pumping.

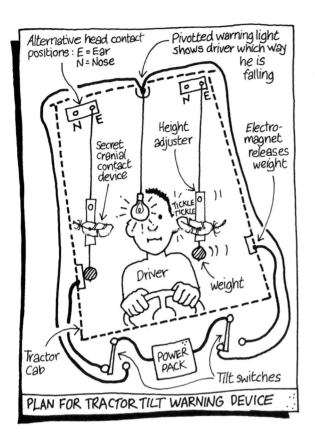

Alternative head contact positions : E = Ear N = Nose

Pivotted warning light shows driver which way he is falling

Height adjuster

Electro-magnet releases weight

Secret cranial contact device

TICKLE TICKLE

Driver

weight

Tractor Cab

POWER PACK

Tilt switches

PLAN FOR TRACTOR TILT WARNING DEVICE

5 Design and make a device that could be fitted to the cab of a tractor to warn the driver when the tractor is dangerously near to the point of rolling over.

6 You are designing a system that will control the locking and unlocking of a door and will warn you of intruders. You have decided to use a set of switches by the door. If the right switches are pressed, the door will unlock, but if anyone tries to break in and presses a wrong switch, the alarm will sound. At this stage, you are trying to design the switches' circuit. The door-locking mechanism is represented by a lamp – when the lamp comes on, it means the door is unlocked, and when the lamp is off, the door is locked. At least three switches should be pressed correctly before the door is unlocked (i.e. the lamp comes on), and if any wrong switch is pressed, a buzzer should sound. (In your final design, you intend to replace the buzzer with a device that opens a trapdoor under the intruder's feet. . .)

EENEY MEENEY MINEY MO...

GET READY ONE COMING

Electronics word search

```
W X T Z A B C O K S T Q E R Y I O L K F G M N B P
A S D F G Y T R W Q U I O P L K J H N M B V C D W
A I O N P O T E N T I O M E T E R P U I H J K E A
P O A J K H O P S D F K L M N E P R E W D S A C X
I K L M O M C D S A G T Y H D J K L P O I M N B H
P O I U M L K J R T F C V I I U I O O C R E T Y U
P O I J K E H O M N B O V I O D F G E U M N B V C
V B N M K J T I O P E I W T D F T D V R T H E P I
F H K L M I O E O E D E R S E I T T E R F R E A S
S T R O C O P M R L E W R B V C E R T E F R U I O
W E R A R A S N A I O N M I A R S T A N R E S N I
I O P P R E S I I R T O N E M N S E R T A M N E E
D A A R O M T H E R M I S T O R I F R I N D T I O
C O O R N N M M R S T T R A I E M I T T E R U R M
W E R E E R N S T T I O R N M S S D V N M E T P E
P O I T R E A N M R I O U M N I Q R W N E E S M N
U I O P O R N M N A W E R S T S E R I E S Q W S D
O P A R A L L E L N E R N S L T O R F O O N M I S
F R I N M N O O I S R E S W V O L T E R T S V F F
W E R S D F G I O I I O N L D R S R S V V M N O U
D C V I S T O R N S P I O N M R V O L T M E T E R
R E E S N V I O P T I O P R N M E E R S B E E R S
A E R S T I O M N O I O R R S M N N D F A G T Y Z
M S I N (B A T T E R Y) E R S N M O O I R S P R E E
P E R S T I O P R U N M S S I O R V V E E A R N M
```

Find these words used in this study of electronics. BATTERY is done for you.

TRANSISTOR	RESISTOR	POTENTIAL DIVIDER
SERIES	PARALLEL	THERMISTOR
CAPACITOR	EMITTER	DIODE
OHM	POTENTIOMETER	AMMETER
CURRENT	LDR	VOLT
VOLTMETER	AMP	BASE

Part 3 Structures

Structures are everywhere!

Wherever you look, you will see examples of **structures**. They occur both in nature and in things made by people to solve particular problems. Here are a few examples.

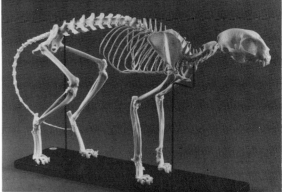

Structures provide **support** – they 'hold things up' against the pull of gravity or other forces acting on them. How good they are at doing this depends on what they are made of, and on their shape.

Optional work

Make a scrapbook of structures found in nature and made by people. Try to match up pictures where a designer or engineer might have used a structure found in nature to solve a problem. For example, the structural design of a VW Beetle is based on that of an eggshell!

1 Structures and forces

1.1 Types of force

A structure provides support. In doing this it is subjected to **forces** which act on it. There are six main types of force which can act on a structure.

1. Tensions or tensile forces

Tension is a 'stretching' force. To show a tensile force acting in a structure, we use arrows like this: ⟵——⟶

2. Compressions or compressive forces

Compression is a 'squashing' force. To show a compressive force acting in a structure we use arrows like this: ⟶——⟵

3. Shear

A **shear** is a force which makes one part of a structure slide past another.

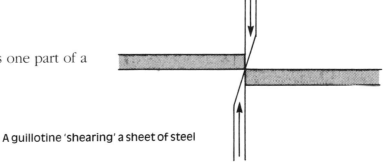

A guillotine 'shearing' a sheet of steel

4. Bending

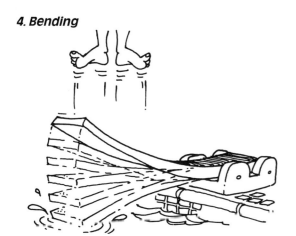

Bending forces can be useful in some structures, but need to be avoided in others!

5. Centrifugal forces

Centrifugal forces occur when an object is revolving around a centre. They 'push' the object away from the centre.

6. Torsion
Torsion is a 'twisting' force

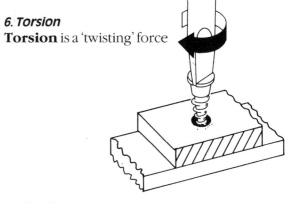

Activity 1

Find examples of structures at home and at school. Draw them and label them with the type of force that acts on them. Try to find at least one example for each type of force.

1.2 Forces acting on a structure

Forces try to alter the shape of the structure they are acting on: if they become too great, they will badly distort the structure and may cause it to collapse. For example, stalks of corn may be knocked down in a hailstorm, an oil rig may collapse in a hurricane, a bone may break in a bad fall. Engineers and technologists need to be able to work out how forces will act on a structure to make sure that the structure will not collapse.

Activity 2

In this activity you will look at the forces acting in a bike frame.

1 Draw a simple diagram of a bike. For example, if your bike looks like this:

draw it like this:

(Try to draw the frame **to scale**.)

2   Make a model of the bike, using straws and pipe-cleaners for the frame and stiff card for the wheels. Use plasticine to make the model stand upright.

A hot glue gun will help to make the joints stronger

3   'Load' the bike by gently pushing down on your model where the saddle would be. (Don't push too hard, or your model will collapse!) Watch carefully what happens to the frame.

4   Draw arrows on your diagram to show the types of force acting on each part of the bike frame. Where are the weak points of the frame?

5   The saddle is not the only place on the frame which will be loaded. Two other places are at the handlebars and at the pedals. Try pushing down gently at these places and see what happens to the frame.

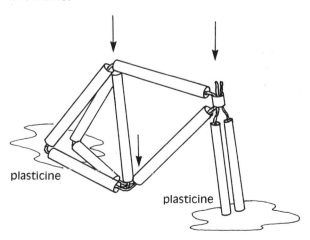

plasticine

plasticine

Framework made from straws and pipecleaners

The classic diamond bike frame – shown here – has been around since about 1890. Many other bike frames have been designed since then. The next activity asks you to look at some of them.

Activity 3

1   Find as many different bike frame designs as you can. Draw simple diagrams of them, and write down what the bike is usually used for. Use arrows on your drawings to show where the loads or forces are applied when someone is riding the bike.

2   Choose three different frames – for example,
● Moulton cycle
● Raleigh Chopper, Grifter or BMX bike
● Itera plastic bike
Make models of the frames as in activity 2.

3   Load the frames as before. Record on your drawings the different forces on each part of the frame.

4   Look at the drawings. Can you suggest why they are similar or different?

Design technology project

Design a new frame for one of these:
● a unisex cycle for shopping
● a track bike
● a racing bike
Draw, make and test your frame as before. Then try to modify your design so that it works better.

SUPA SHOPPA

2 Columns and beams

Many structures are made from **beams** joined together to make **frameworks**. In this section you are going to look at how beams can resist forces acting on them.

2.1 Resisting a compressive force

Activity 4

For this activity, you need A4 sheets of paper, scissors, sticky tape, ruler, two pieces of hardboard or stiff card, 120 mm square, and gram masses.

1 Roll an A4 sheet of paper into a tube 210 mm long. Tape the seam, making sure that there is no overlap. Measure the diameter of the tube, and write it down.

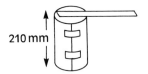

Put the pieces of card at the top and the bottom of the tube. Carefully load the tube with gram masses until it collapses. Work out the force in newtons that made the tube collapse (this is roughly equal to 10 times the total mass in kilograms). Draw a sketch of how the tube collapsed.

2 Repeat step 1 several times, using a smaller diameter each time.

Keep the tube walls the same thickness each time.

You might like to write your results in a table.

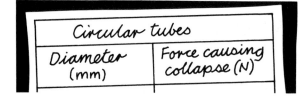

Circular tubes	
Diameter (mm)	Force causing collapse (N)

3 Did you find that changing the diameter of the tube (but not its length) affected its ability to withstand a compressive force? Write down what you discovered. Try drawing a graph. Use axes like these.

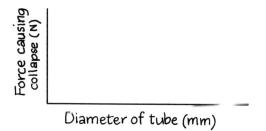

Activity 5

Repeat activity 4, but use **square** section tubes, then **corrugated** tubes. Write about what you discover.

Are you sure we've got the right size paper?

2.2 Resisting a bending force

Activity 6

You need a strip of balsa wood 300 mm × 25 mm × 3 mm, 0.2 kg mass, two rulers, and blocks or plasticine for support.

1 Make a gap of 280 mm between two benches. Put the balsa wood strip across the gap like this.

Hang the mass from the centre of the strip. Measure how much the strip bends.

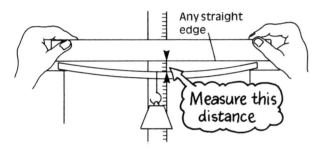

Any straight edge

Measure this distance

2 Turn the strip on its edge. Use blocks or plasticine to support it. Repeat step 1.

Only 10mm should be supported at each end

3 In which position was the strip more able to resist the bending force? Why?

4 When the strip was in this position, did you find that another type of force was present? Repeat the test, increasing the load if necessary. Write down what you see.

Designers and engineers have worked out different ways of reducing the weight of a beam without reducing its strength. There are two main ways of doing this. One is to make the beam from a modern material which is light in weight yet very strong. Another way is to change the shape of the beam's **section**.

A bike frame is a tube and would look like this if you sawed it in half.

Section of bike frame

The diagram below shows common steel girder sections. These sections have been devised by engineers to reduce weight while retaining strength, and to minimise twisting caused by torsional forces.

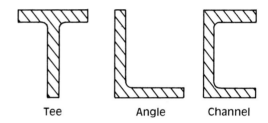

Tee   Angle   Channel

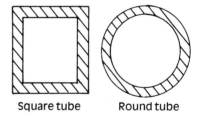

Square tube   Round tube

Activity 7

Think about what happened to the balsa strip in activity 6 when you turned it on its edge. Try to make a beam section using balsa wood that will resist bending **and** torsional forces. Test it as before.

Activity 8

1 Make a gap of 260 mm between two benches. Shape, fold, and glue a sheet of A4 paper into a beam. Put the paper beam across the gap.

2 Carefully load the beam at its centre, using small gram masses. Increase the load gradually until the beam collapses. Record this load.

3 Compare your results with those of your friends. Whose beam withstood the greatest load? What do you notice about the most successful design?

2.3 What happens when beams bend?

Designers and engineers need to understand what happens when beams bend under a load, so that they can work out how to minimise the bending. In the next activity you will find out what happens to a beam as it bends.

Activity 9

You need a piece of polystyrene foam 400 mm × 50 mm × 20 mm, a ruler, a felt-tip pen and a tape measure.

1 Draw a line down the middle of the widest side of the foam. Draw lines 20 mm apart, at 90° to the centre line.

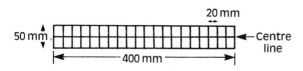

2 Bend the foam so that there is a deflection of about 40 mm in the middle.

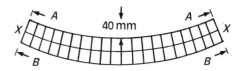

Use the tape measure to measure the distance A–A, X–X and B–B. Write them down.

3 What do you notice about the distances A–A, X–X and B–B, compared with the original length of the foam? Use the words below to complete this paragraph:

> When a beam bends under a load, the top surface _____ and experiences a _____. The bottom surface _____ and experiences a _____. The centre of the beam _____.

Words to use
stays the same length
is stretched
is squeezed
compression
tension

What you found in activity 9 happens in all beams. The centre of a beam – the part that stays the same length – is called the **neutral axis**. Beams resist bending more when their material is further from the neutral axis. This is why the strip of balsa in activity 6 bent less when it was put on its edge.

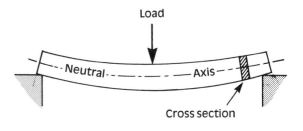

Look for beams in your school and other buildings. Are they used 'edge-on'?

2.4 Reinforcing beams

Many modern buildings like office blocks and multi-storey car-parks use frameworks of concrete beams. Concrete cannot be stretched – it cracks! But you found in activity 9 that the bottom edge of all beams experiences a tension – a stretching force. To solve this problem, engineers **reinforce** the concrete beam. Steel rods are put into the concrete when it is being made into beams. The position of the rods in the beam is very important. You will find out more about this in the next activity.

Activity 10

1 Make a mould like this from wood. The measurements on the diagram are in mm.

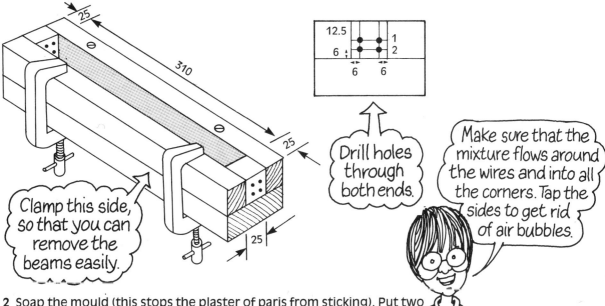

Drill holes through both ends.

Make sure that the mixture flows around the wires and into all the corners. Tap the sides to get rid of air bubbles.

Clamp this side, so that you can remove the beams easily.

2 Soap the mould (this stops the plaster of paris from sticking). Put two welding rod wires through the bottom two holes of the end blocks. Pour runny plaster of paris into the mould. When the beam has set, take it out of the mould.

3 Make another beam with the wires in the bottom two holes. When you turn this upside down, the rods will be in the top half of the beam!

4 Make a third beam, but with the wires in the centre.

5 Leave the beams to harden for 24 hours.

6 Use this set-up to test each beam.

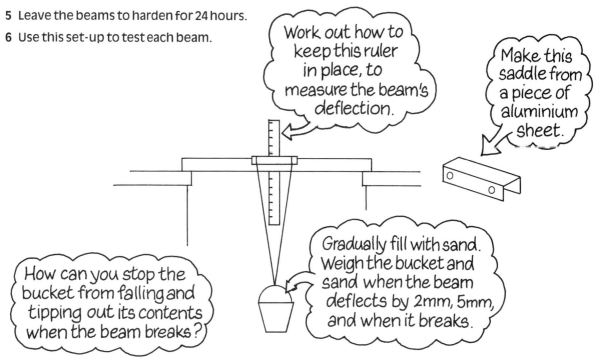

Record your results in a table like this.

Beam Reinforced –	Force (N) causing		
	2 mm deflection	5 mm deflection	Fracture
– in the top half			
– in the centre			
– in the bottom half			

7 Where would rods be put in a concrete beam to reinforce it?

2.5 Preventing bending in bridge beams

The longer the beam, the more chance there is of it bending when it is loaded. This becomes very important when the beam is part of a bridge, for example. However, engineers have worked out ways of transferring loads and forces from the centre of a bridge to its supports. Extra parts – called **struts** and **ties** – are used.

Struts transfer **compressive** forces.

Ties transfer **tensile** forces.

Activity 11 looks at how these can be used in a bridge.

46

Activity 11

Materials needed

- Two sheets of balsa wood, 310 mm × 60 mm × 1 mm
- Three strips of balsa wood, 360 mm × 4 mm square
- Scraps of card
- Button thread
- Eight paper clips
- Hot glue gun and mapping pins

1 Place two house bricks 300 mm apart, and put a sheet of balsa on them. Carefully load the sheet with gram masses until the balsa deflects by 5 mm. Record the total load in grams.

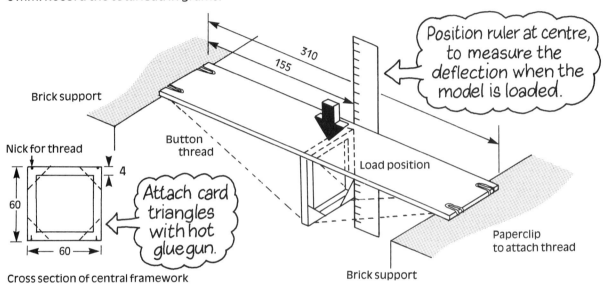

Brick support

310

155

Position ruler at centre, to measure the deflection when the model is loaded.

Nick for thread

Button thread

Load position

4

60

Attach card triangles with hot glue gun.

60

Paperclip to attach thread

Cross section of central framework

Brick support

2 Make a model bridge, as in the diagram above. Test the model bridge as in step 1. What do you notice about the load needed to cause a deflection of 5 mm?

3 Are the threads experiencing tensile or compressive forces? Are they struts or ties? What kind of forces are being transferred by the framework in the centre?

4 Now turn your model upside down and try to load it again. What happens? What forces are being transferred to the threads now?

In a real bridge, the threads would be steel ropes or chains. This activity shows that engineers cannot use ropes or chains where there are compressive forces.

5 If your original bridge were built over a canal, the central framework and the ties would get in the way of the boats using the canal. Try to build a bridge using the same basic design, but with the central framework **above** the bridge. Use only the materials provided.

6 Test your new design as in step 1. Is this bridge stronger than the other?

47

3 Frameworks

Large structures are often **frameworks** of beams. Many modern office blocks are steel frame constructions, with the gaps filled in with bricks, panels and glass. Many railway bridges and cranes are examples of **open** steel frame structures. Some pieces of furniture are frame structures.

3.1 Rigid frameworks

The framework of a structure must be able to resist the various forces acting on it – it must remain **rigid** and not collapse when it is used. In this section you will be looking at how rigid frameworks can be designed and made.

Activity 12

1 Use four flat strips from a construction kit to make a square frame. Tighten up the screws and nuts at the corners. Try to push the square in across a diagonal. Does the framework stay the same shape? That is, does it resist compressive forces well?

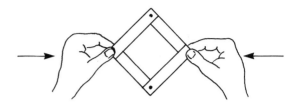

2 Stop pushing across the diagonal. Does the framework go back to its original shape?

3 Modify the square frame by adding struts or ties so that the frame will resist a fairly strong compressive force across either diagonal. Keep your design as simple as possible.

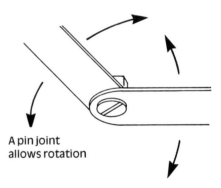

A pin joint allows rotation

In the last activity you used small screws and nuts to join individual beams together to make a framework – you used **pin joints**. Pin joints are useful when you are trying to design rigid frameworks because they allow rotation. If your framework is rigid when you try it out using pin joints, it will remain rigid when you make the final structure using strong joints which do not allow rotation.

Gusset plates are often used to strengthen joints in large structures like bridges and cranes.

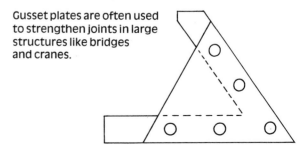

Activity 13

Which shapes are rigid even when pin joints are used? Find out in this activity.

1 Use flat strips from a construction kit, together with screws and nuts, to make a variety of flat shapes. For example, you could make hexagons, quadrilaterals, triangles, and so on. Make them using pin joints at the corners.

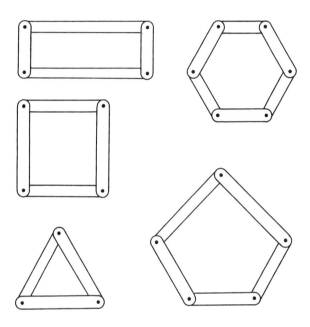

2 Sketch each shape, then subject each to a small compressive or tensile force. Write 'rigid' or 'not rigid' by your sketch.

3 Which shape is rigid even when pin joints are used?

This shape is used a lot in structures which have to withstand large forces. Look at the photographs at the start of this section, for example.

Design technology project

Design and construct a flat open framework 300 mm long and 80 mm high. ('Open' means that your design must not fill in the rectangle – it must be an open framework which you can see through.)

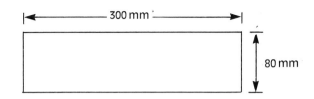

These are the only materials you can use:
- strips of balsa wood 150 mm × 6 mm square
- string or twine
- stiff card or hardboard

A hot glue gun is useful for making the framework.

...but none of these strips are long enough.

Test your framework across a gap of 280 mm, using a method like that shown in activity 10, step 6.

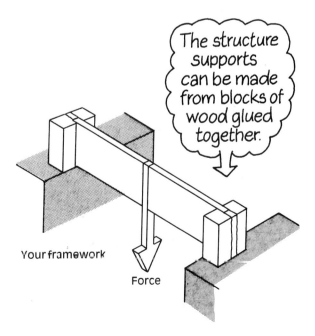

The structure supports can be made from blocks of wood glued together.

Your framework

Force

3.2 Truss structures

The framework you made and tested in design technology project 2 was an open flat framework. It was also an example of a **truss** – a framework whose overall length is longer than the length of any beam used to make it. Here is another example of a truss.

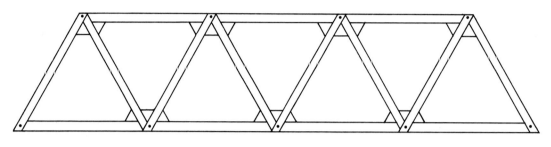

Individual trusses are 'two-dimensional'; they have length and width but very little thickness. Because of this they can be affected by torsional, twisting forces. (Did this happen to your framework when you tested it?) Engineers solve these torsional problems by joining flat frameworks together to make a three-dimensional structure like a crane jib or a bridge.

Examples of truss bridges can be found on many railway systems throughout the world. Most of the designs were developed during the last century, when the railways in Western Europe and North America were expanding rapidly. They were built using wood, or iron and steel, depending on what materials were available.

Look out for truss bridges as you travel around. Here are some of the more common designs.

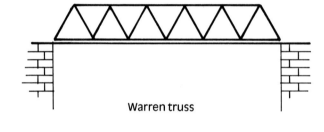

Warren truss

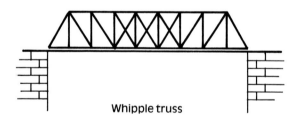

Whipple truss

What shape is used in all of these designs? Why?

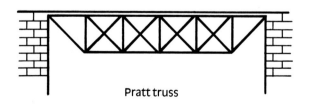

Pratt truss

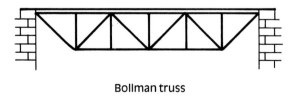

Bollman truss

4 Spanning gaps

Designers and engineers often have to devise a method of **spanning a gap**. Sometimes the gap is small (for example, a doorway in a house), but the gap can also be very large (for example, a very wide river). In section 3.2 you saw one solution to the problem of spanning a gap – truss bridges. A number of other solutions have been devised. This section looks at some of them.

4.1 Cantilevers

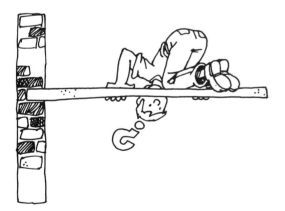

A **cantilever** is a beam which has one end built into a rigid support called an **encastre**. The other end of the beam is not supported. Ancient Chinese civilisations used cantilevers in building bridges.

Activity 14

NO GLUE ALLOWED

1 Use blocks of wood 70 mm × 25 mm × 15 mm to build a bridge like the one above. How wide a gap can you span like this?

2 Think about the problems you had in building your bridge. Try to work out ways of overcoming these problems. (Hint: think about what a cantilever is.)

4.2 Arches

Arches are frequently used to span gaps. About 5000 years ago, Egyptian and Sumerian engineers used **corbelled arches** in their buildings. The bridge you built in activity 14 is an example of a corbelled arch.

Corbelled arch

Another way of building an arch is to use wedge-shaped blocks called **voussoirs**. Sometimes the voussoir at the top of the arch – the **keystone** – is larger than the others. The supports each side of the arch are called **abutments**.

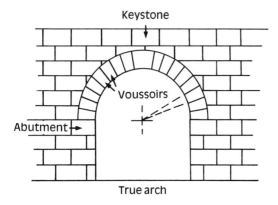

True arch

An arch will not fall down if it is supported at the sides. This is because the design of the arch changes the direction of the forces acting on it, like this.

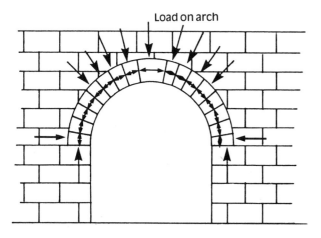

Activity 15

In this activity you are going to make a model arch. Use wood, plasticine, clay or expanded polystyrene to make the voussoirs.

1 Make a card **template** of the voussoir shape.

2 Use the template to make nine voussoirs. These must be made accurately, or your arch will fall down.

3 Stick two voussoirs to the base to form the abutments. Then build the arch.

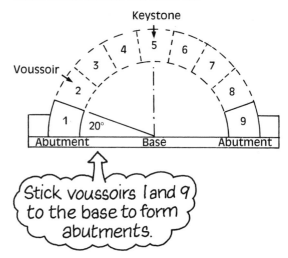

Stick voussoirs 1 and 9 to the base to form abutments.

4 Find out what happens to your arch when you load it in these positions.

Work out your own way of loading the arch in each of these positions. Try not to break it!

4.3 Suspension bridges

Suspension bridges can be used to span very wide gaps. For example, the Humber bridge spans a gap of 1410 metres.

Activity 16

In this activity you and four of your friends will find out what it feels like to be part of a suspension bridge! You need about 4 metres of rope and some padding.

1 Set up your bridge like this. Take turns to be each part of the bridge.

2 Draw and label a line diagram of the bridge. Draw arrows to show the forces experienced by each part of the bridge.

5 Forces acting in a structure

5.1 Identifying the kinds of forces

In section 1 you looked at the six different types of force that can act on a structure, and tried to work out the different kinds acting on a bike frame by building a model and testing it.

Another way of working this out is to draw the structure as a line diagram with pin joints, which will allow the lines to rotate. Here is an example.

To find out whether a beam is in tension or in compression, you imagine what would happen to the structure **if that particular beam were removed**.

Let's find out what force beam *AB* is experiencing.

To find out what force *AB* is experiencing, first remove it.

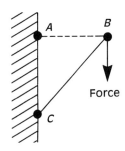

What would happen now to beam *BC*?

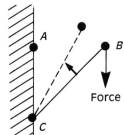

Would it move upwards?

Or would it move downwards?

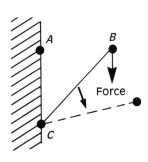

If *AB* were removed, beam *BC* would move downwards. So beam *AB* must be experiencing a **tensile** force. Label the line diagram with ▸━━━━◂ arrows.

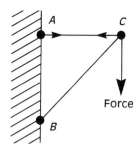

Activity 17

1 Copy the line diagram. Work out what kind of force beam *BC* is experiencing. Show it on your diagram.

2 Is beam *AB* a strut or a tie?

3 Is beam *BC* a strut or a tie?

5.2 Distribution of forces

Engineers and designers need to work out how the forces applied to a structure are distributed in it. This can be done by quite complicated calculations based on the practical ideas in the next activity. The structure you will investigate is:

Activity 18

1 Find a strip of softwood 420 mm × 30 mm × 10 mm. Mark it like this, and drill a small hole 10 mm from each end.

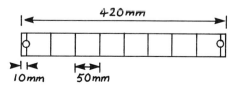

2 Hold the strip (the beam) horizontal using two newton-meters. Write down the reading of each newton-meter. Is the weight of the beam distributed evenly or unevenly? (Are the readings on the newton-meters the same or different?)

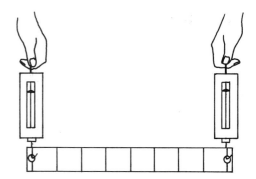

3 Make a table like this.

Distance of load from centre	Left-hand reading (N)	Right-hand reading (N)
No load		
At centre		
100 mm to left		
150 mm to left		
100 mm to right		
150 mm to right		

Record your readings in a table like this

Hang a 1 kg mass from the centre of the beam. This is a load force of about 10 newtons. Record the readings of the newton-meters in the table.

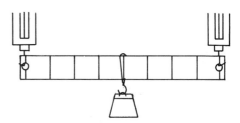

4 Move the mass to this position and note the readings of the meters.

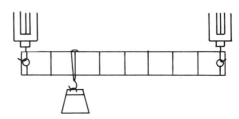

5 Now move the mass here, and record the new readings.

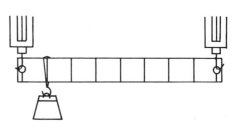

6 Repeat steps 4 and 5 to the right of the beam's centre.

7 Look at your table. Write about what you notice. For example, how is the load distributed when it is at the centre of the beam? What happens when the load is moved away from the centre? And so on.

This activity shows several things:

1 The weight of the beam on its own is distributed **evenly**. Both newton-meters recorded the same force.

2 When the load is at the centre of the beam, the force is distributed **evenly**. Once again, both newton-meters recorded the same force.

3 When the load is moved away from the centre, the force is distributed **unevenly**. The newton-meters recorded different forces.

4 The further the load is moved away from the centre (and the closer it is to one end of the beam), the greater the difference between the readings on the two meters.

You may have met these ideas before in science lessons. They are known as the **principle of moments**, and are used by engineers and designers to calculate the distribution of forces in structures.

Design technology projects

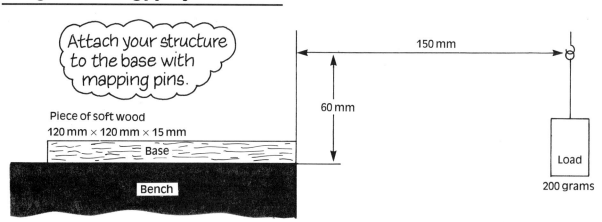

1 Imagine you are a structural engineer. Your company has been asked to work out a way of supporting a load. The structure must be cheap to build, and use as little material as possible. Design and build a scale model of the structure, using straws, pipe-cleaners and thread, to meet these requirements.

The diagram shows the detailed requirements, and the base you should use for your model.

Estimate how much the real structure would cost to build, from the materials used in your model. The costs of the materials are:
- Straws   £20 per 10 mm
- Pipe-cleaners   £15 per 10 mm
- Thread   £10 per 10 mm
- Pins   £50 each

2 Design and build a model bridge to support a road 50 mm wide and to span a gap of 300 mm. You can use only the following materials:
● 7 lengths of balsa wood, 600 mm × 5 mm square
● 1 length of card, 400 mm × 50 mm × 0.25 mm

(for the roadway and gusset plates)
● Hot glue gun, mapping pins and modelling knife

Test the strength of your bridge as in activity 10.

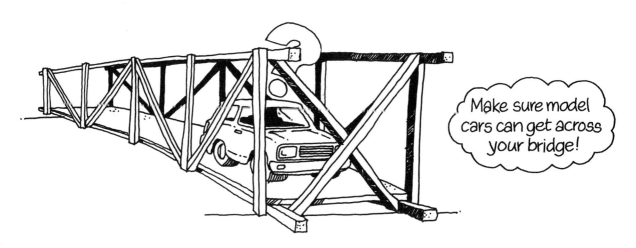

Make sure model cars can get across your bridge!

3 Imagine you are a furniture designer. Your company wants a design for a patio chair. It is to be cut from a single piece of plywood, then steam-bent and glued to make the chair.

Design a pattern for a chair on a piece of 5 mm grid paper, 100 mm by 200 mm. Cut out your pattern, and fold and glue it together.

Here is an example pattern and chair.

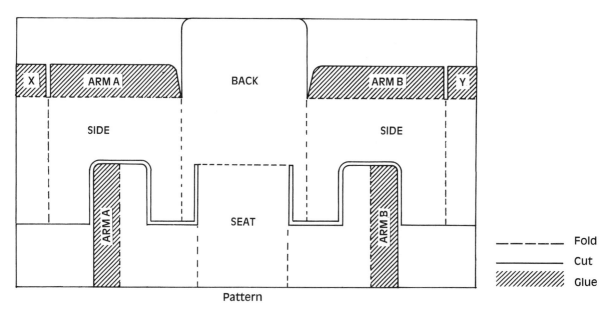

Pattern

------- Fold
——— Cut
////// Glue

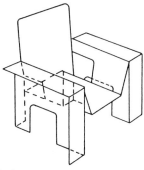

Completed chair

Use gram masses to test your chair. Find out what load it will support.

What other things – apart from strength – are important to think about when designing a chair? Can you test your chair for these aspects?

Structures word search

```
C L O C K W I S E A (S T R U C T U R E) I S A D D
B E A M E V I K E W H I C Z P D O V I T E S I S
U C N P O R T W A T H O U T S U R P D R T G E V
E O Y T E N S I O N T H S N G W O Y L D I F A L
L M O W R N I T O S I M P M R T A N T R W H L N
T P B N K O N I A A N T I C L O C K W I S E O U
T R T R U C S T U R E S N O E T T O S T M P B Y
W E Q N K S F U T H E M A S O N L Y M A N M A E
D S W E E R E S G U R Z O U N D T E D R Y L C O
T S O R E X A N M A P L E S O F R R N A T R U R
A I S T U C I T U R L E S W E L U E I R O N A L
O O F R O D M I R T H E R N A T S U R F E A B I
C N C L N E W T O N M E T R E S S E F R U A M E
V A N K G G S R H I L L G I V U E U S T X G T R
O A B F O A M I E W O S R K S S L O S K A T A T
U H E E N V I A R O N H M E N P T T O A N S T L
S W E R Q U E N S T I E O N S E Q D A L I T O Y
S O F C O N S G T R U A C T I N O N C A N A R F
O M C A N T I L E V E R F F E S C T S T R S S N
I G O H T A N E D Q U O D T I I L A T E N R I A
R L S M A R E N O T S T A B L O E T H O E Y O T
E N D T E O F R A M E W O R K N C O T L A L N A
P S E S G N D E W A Y S J O V N I W N G D R I F
F E R E N T T M A T E S I A L S E C A N B E C A
P N E W T O N S T H B N K B E N D I N G O F A H
```

Find the following terms and words used in this study of structures e.g. STRUCTURE is done for you.

BEAM
TENSION
COMPRESSION
SHEAR
BENDING
ARCH
TORSION
CENTRIFUGAL
NEWTONS
FORCE
FRAMEWORK
TRIANGLE
SUSPENSION
RIGID
TRUSS
MOMENTS
CANTILEVER
VOUSSOIR

Part 4 Mechanisms

Machines, mechanisms and movement

The technological advances people have made through the ages have been closely linked with their ability to harness energy and use it to perform **mechanical work**. Mechanical work is done by a **machine**, which converts (changes) or transmits (passes on) energy. Machines are made from a number of working parts called **mechanisms**. A mechanism changes an **input** force and movement into a desired **output** force and movement.

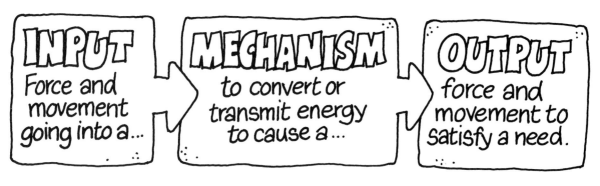

INPUT Force and movement going into a... > MECHANISM to convert or transmit energy to cause a... > OUTPUT force and movement to satisfy a need.

All mechanisms are based on what ancient philosophers called **the mighty five**. This was their description of the five simple machines which form the basis of all the other machines developed throughout history.

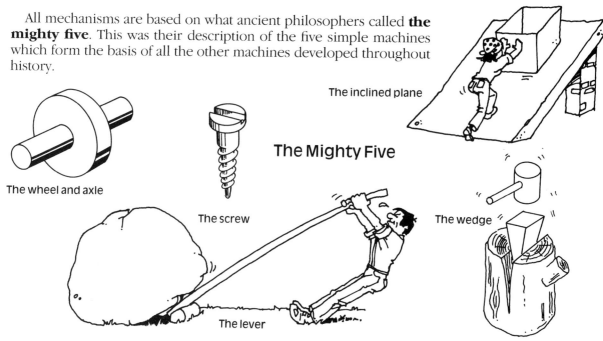

The inclined plane

The wheel and axle

The screw

The Mighty Five

The wedge

The lever

Engineers through the ages have used the principles of 'the mighty five' to build machines which gradually became more and more complex as the problems they were trying to solve became more difficult and demanding.

Some modern mechanisms seem very difficult – if not impossible – to understand because they are so complex. But if you examine them closely, you will find that they are simply very ingenious adaptations of 'the mighty five'.

Mechanisms can be described by the kind of motion they produce. There are four types.

1. Linear motion

Movement in a straight line in one direction only is called **linear motion**. Linear motion is shown in diagrams as ⟶

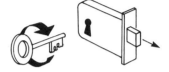

When a key is turned in a lock, the lock mechanism changes the input rotary motion into an output linear motion.

2. Reciprocating motion

Movement backwards and forwards in a straight line is called **reciprocating motion**. It is shown in diagrams as ⟵⟶

A piston moving up and down a cylinder is an example of reciprocating motion. (The lock mechanism is **not** an example of reciprocating motion, even though it will move backward and forward. Can you think why it is not?)

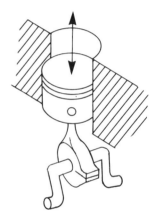

3. Rotary motion

Circular movement is called **rotary motion**, and is drawn in diagrams as ↺

There are several examples of rotary motion in a bicycle.

4. Oscillating motion

Forward and backward movement in an arc (part of a circle) is called **oscillating motion**. It is shown in diagrams as ⤵⤴

A clock pendulum is an example of oscillating motion.

Optional work

Try to think of some more examples showing the different kinds of
motion. Note down the input motion and the output motion for each
example. For example, think about sewing machines, hand drills, car
windows, kitchen scales, and so on.

1   Levers

1.1 Introducing levers

A **lever** is a stiff rod that pivots (turns) about a point. The point is called
a **fulcrum**. The input force (the **effort**) and motion is transmitted
through the lever to move the **load**.

Activity 1

In this activity you are going to make a model which can be used to find
out more about levers. It can be made from wood, metal or plastic strips.

1 Mark and cut out three strips like these. (Note: the scale of this
diagram is **half full size**. The measurements, in millimetres, are for the
full size strips.)

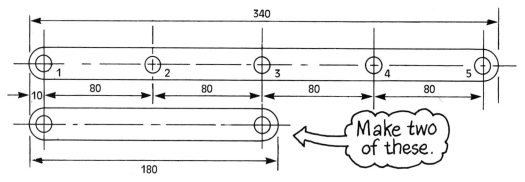

2 Put your model together like this. Clamp it in a vice.

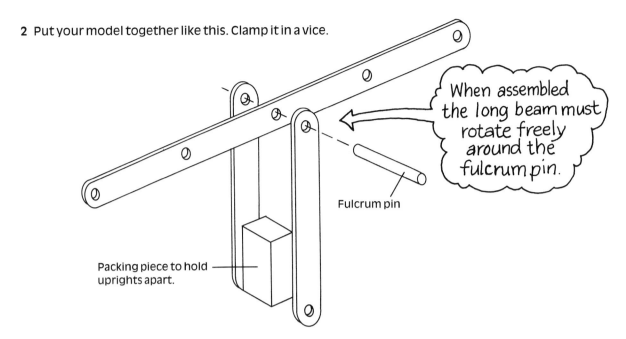

When assembled the long beam must rotate freely around the fulcrum pin.

Fulcrum pin

Packing piece to hold uprights apart.

3 Hang a newton-meter at each end of the long beam (holes 1 and 5). The beam should 'balance'. If it doesn't, modify it.

4 Hold the left meter still, using one finger. (This is the load.) Gently pull down the other meter, again using one finger. (This is the effort.) Write down the readings on **both** meters.

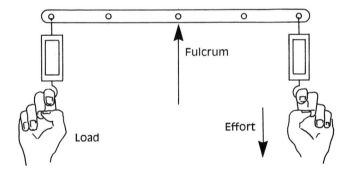

Fulcrum

Effort

Load

5 Remove the newton-meters, and then modify your model by moving the fulcrum to hole 2.

Move the fulcrum to here.

6 Put the newton-meters back. The beam will not balance now! Gently pull down on the left-hand meter until the beam is horizontal. Read the meter and write down the force needed to make the beam horizontal.

7 Repeat stage 4 with the fulcrum at hole 4.

8 Repeat stage 4 again, but this time hold the right-hand meter steady (the load) and apply the effort force through the left meter.

9 Look at your results. Write about what you notice. (For example, is the effort less than, equal to or greater than the load? Does it matter where the fulcrum is? And so on.)

1.2 Type 1 levers

There are three different kinds of lever, called type 1, type 2 and type 3. The model you used in activity 1 is an example of a type 1 lever.

A **type 1 lever** has the fulcrum (the pivot point) between the effort and the load.

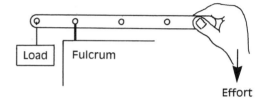

Activity 2

Use the model you made in activity 1 to try these out.

1 Hang a 100 g mass at the end of the beam nearest the fulcrum. The mass provides a load force of about 1 newton. Push down on the other end of the beam to raise the load. Try to remember how much effort it takes to raise the load. Note how far the load moves compared with how far the effort moves.

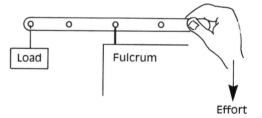

2 Move the fulcrum to the centre of the beam. Use the same mass as load. Raise the load as before. How much effort is needed this time as compared with last time? Again, note how far the load moves compared with how far the effort moves.

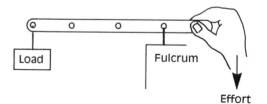

3 Move the fulcrum again, and use the same load. Raise the load as before. How much effort is needed this time, compared with that needed in steps 1 and 2? How far does the load move, compared with how far the effort moves?

4 Think about your results. Try to explain how the position of the fulcrum affects
• the effort needed to move the load, and
• the distance the load moves compared to the distance the effort moves.

Activity 3

Here are examples of type 1 levers in action. Sketch them and label the fulcrum, load and effort positions for each one.

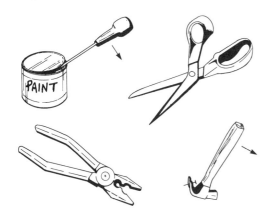

1.3 Type 2 levers

Type 2 levers have the load between the fulcrum and the effort.

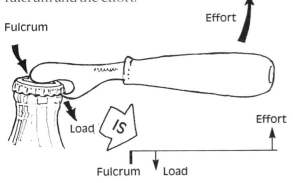

Activity 4

In this activity you will use the model you made in activity 1 as a type 2 lever. Make a table like this before you start.

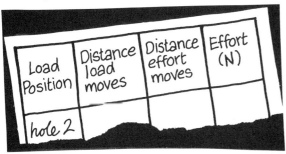

1 Set up the fulcrum pin at hole 1. Hang a 100 g mass at hole 2, as shown in the diagram. Attach a newton-meter to hole 5. The meter will be used to measure the effort.

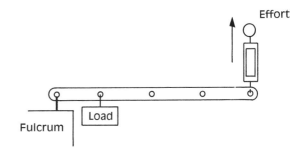

2 Raise the load by lifting the newton-meter. Write down in the table the effort needed. Find a way of measuring the distances moved by the load and the effort, and write these results in the table.

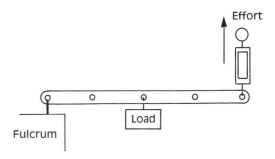

3 Move the load to hole 3, and repeat step 2 for this position.

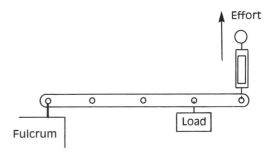

4 Move the load to hole 4. **Before** you repeat step 2, try to **predict** how much effort will be needed to raise the load and the distances moved by the load and the effort. (Look at your results so far.) Then **test** your prediction by repeating step 2. Was your prediction correct?

1.4 Type 3 levers

Type 3 levers have the effort between the fulcrum and the load.

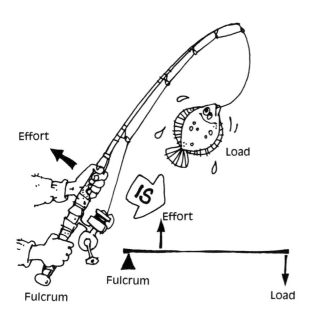

Activity 5

In this activity you will use the model as a type 3 lever. Make a table like this before you start.

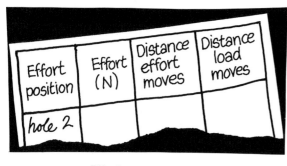

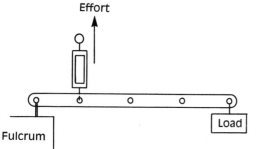

1 Set up the fulcrum at hole 1 and hang the 100 g mass from hole 5. Attach the newton-meter to hole 2, as shown.

2 Raise the load by lifting the newton-meter. Write in the table the effort force needed. Measure the distances moved by the load and by the effort, and write these results in the table.

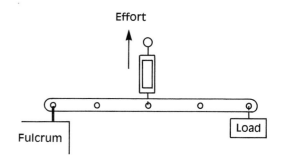

3 Move the newton-meter to hole 3. Repeat step 2 for this position of the effort.

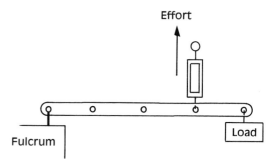

4 Move the newton-meter to hole 4. **Before** you repeat step 2, try to **predict** how much effort will be needed to raise the load and the distances moved by the load and the effort. (Look at your results so far.) Then test your prediction by repeating step 2. Was your prediction correct?

1.5 Mechanical advantage

Did you find in the previous activities that the effort needed to lift the load was sometimes **less** than the load? When this happens, the lever (the beam) must be **magnifying** the smaller effort to enable it to lift the larger load. This magnification is called the **mechanical**

advantage (M.A.) of the lever. The mechanical advantage of a lever can be worked out by using this formula:

$$M.A. = Load \div Effort \text{ or } \frac{Load}{Effort}$$

Here is an example.

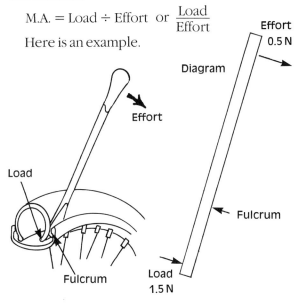

A punctured bike tyre exerts a force of 1.5 newtons on the rim of the wheel. It is levered off by an effort of 0.5 newton on the tyre lever.

$$M.A. = Load \div Effort$$
$$= 1.5 \div 0.5$$
$$= 3$$

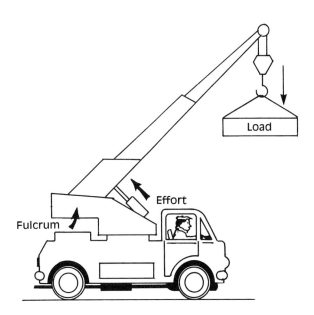

Activity 6

Work out the mechanical advantages of these levers.

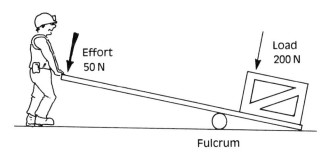

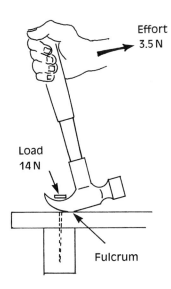

The load is always nearer to the fulcrum than the effort in levers that gain a mechanical advantage.

What do you notice about the mechanical advantage of the crane? What kind of lever is it?

Activity 7

Look back at your results for activities 1, 4 and 5. Find the levers which gained a mechanical advantage, and use your results to work out the M.A. in each case.

Optional work

1 Theoretically, identical levers should gain the same mechanical advantage, but in practice they often do not. Compare the mechanical advantages you got for your lever with those obtained by your friends' levers. Can you think what might affect the mechanical advantage gained by a particular lever?

2 Although you can lift a larger load with a smaller effort using a lever which gains a mechanical advantage, you have to pay for it! The distance moved by the effort is greater than the distance the load moves. Is this true for your levers?

3 Other mechanisms can also gain a mechanical advantage. Try calculating the mechanical advantage of this pulley system. You may need to refer to the section on pulleys and sprockets on p72.

Section of Support

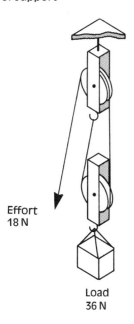

Effort
18 N

Load
36 N

1.6 Velocity ratio

Did you find that in many levers the distance moved by the effort is different from the distance moved by the load? The relationship between these two distances is called the **velocity ratio (V.R.)**. You can work it out by using this formula:

$$\text{V.R.} = \frac{\text{Distance moved by effort (input)}}{\text{Distance moved by load (output)}}$$

In levers where the velocity ratio is greater than 1, the effort (the input) moves further than the load (the output). For levers with a velocity ratio less than 1, the output motion is greater than the input motion.

Activity 8

Look at your results for activities 1, 4 and 5. Work out the velocity ratio for each lever.

Optional work

What price do you have to pay in systems that produce a large output motion for a small input motion? Write down what you think.

Design problem
'Lift the anvil'

2 Linkages

2.1 Using levers in linkages

Pop-up book

Windscreen wipers

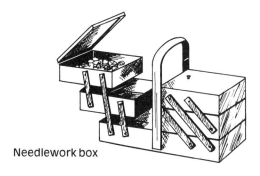
Needlework box

Levers can be joined together to make **linkages**. Linkages, like levers and other mechanisms, change an **input motion and force** into an **output motion and force**.

Activity 9

Use Meccano or a similar construction kit for this and the following activities.

1 Make this linkage, using three flat strips together with screws and bolts for the lose pins.

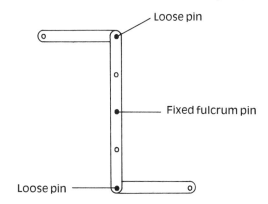
Loose pin
Fixed fulcrum pin
Loose pin

2 Attach the linkage to a flat piece of plywood, using a round-headed screw (the fixed fulcrum pin) and two washers.

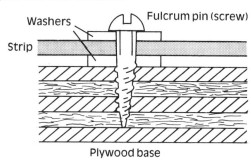
Washers
Fulcrum pin (screw)
Strip
Plywood base

3 Push strip A like this. Write down how the linkage alters the input motion. Does it change the direction of the input motion? Does it increase or reduce the distance of the input motion?

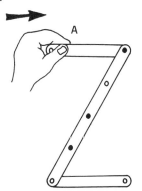
A

4 Attach newton-meters as shown here. Hold meter B still while applying some force and movement through meter A. Write down the readings on both meters. What do you notice?

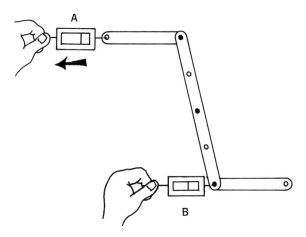

A

B

This linkage reverses the input motion as the central lever pivots around the fixed fulcrum. The input and output forces are the same, because the fulcrum is at the centre of the central lever.

Activity 10

Use the linkage of activity 9 to do these.

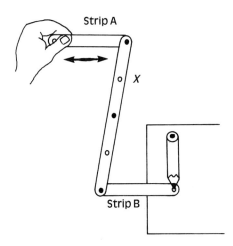

Strip A

X

Strip B

1 Put some paper under strip B, and fit a pencil point through one of the strip's holes.

2 Put a small reciprocating motion into the linkage through strip A. Does the output motion

– recorded by the pencil – reverse and amplify the input motion? Or does it reverse and reduce it?

3 Move the fixed fulcrum to X and repeat step 2. What happens now?

Activity 11

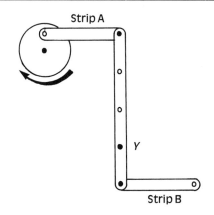

Strip A

Y

Strip B

1 Move the fixed fulcrum to Y. Attach a wheel to the end of strip A. Turn the wheel. Record the output motion.

2 Put a reciprocating motion into the linkage through strip B. What happens?

Optional work

1 Make these linkages. Apply the input motion shown, and record the output motion(s).

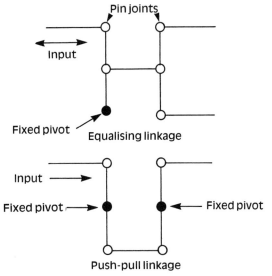

Pin joints

Input

Fixed pivot   Equalising linkage

Input

Fixed pivot   Fixed pivot

Push-pull linkage

2 If you put guide blocks to both the input and the output strips of the linkage in activity 9 to stop them 'flapping', the linkage will jam when you try to put motion through it.

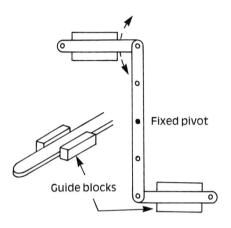

Fixed pivot

Guide blocks

(a) Try to explain why the linkage jams.
(b) Modify the system so that it will work with the guide blocks in place.

2.2 Applications of linkages

Here are some examples of linkages in use. Try them out for yourself.

A trammel linkage
This is for drawing parallel lines.

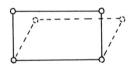

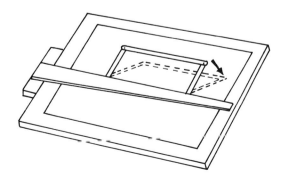

A pantograph linkage
If you want to enlarge a drawing, you can use a pantograph linkage.

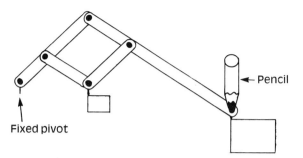

Pencil

Fixed pivot

Extending tongs linkage

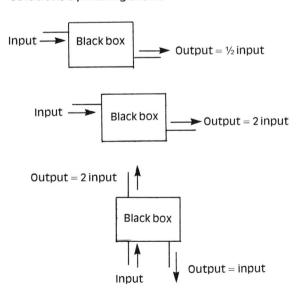

Optional work

The 'black boxes' hide different linkages. Work out what the linkages must be. Check your solutions by making them.

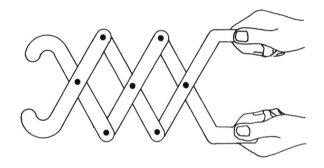

Input → Black box → Output = ½ input

Input → Black box → Output = 2 input

Output = 2 input ↑   Black box   Input ↑   Output = input ↓

71

Design technology project

Design and make a funny face with moving parts – eyes that cross, ears that waggle, a tongue that sticks out, and so on.

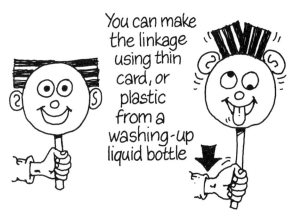

You can make the linkage using thin card, or plastic from a washing-up liquid bottle

3 Pulleys and sprockets

3.1 Pulleys

Pulleys are used to change the direction of an input force, or to gain a mechanical advantage, or both.

In the activities in this section you will need to suspend different pulley systems from a tower and jib. Activity 12 asks you to design and build a tower and jib, using your knowledge of structures (section 3).

Activity 12

Design and build a tower and jib using a construction kit or any other suitable materials. The tower, which will be anchored in a vice, must be at least 150 mm high. The jib reach must be at least 150 mm.

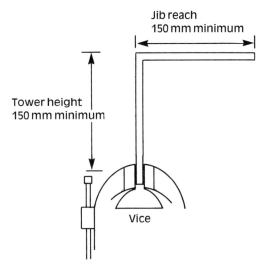

Your construction must be strong enough to support a pulley system on the end of the jib being used to raise a load of 5 newtons.

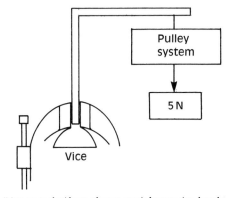

(Your solution does not have to look like the diagrams above. In fact, you will need to use extra struts and ties to make the structure rigid.)

Activity 13

1 Attach a pulley wheel to the end of the jib. Tie a 0.5 kg mass (to act as the load) on a piece of string. Pass the string over the pulley, and tie a newton-meter to the other end.

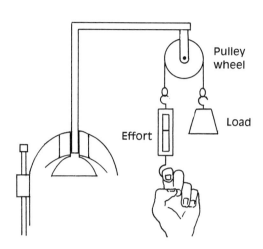

2 Raise the load by pulling down on the newton-meter. Read and record the effort force needed. Is it the same as the load (about 5 newtons), or more, or less?

3 Stop raising the load, but leave it hanging. Read and record the effort needed to hold this state of **equilibrium**. Is it the same as the load, or more, or less?

4 Does this pulley system gain a mechanical advantage?

REMEMBER! M.A. = Load / Effort

Although the pulley system in activity 13 raises a load, it does not gain a mechanical advantage – the effort force needed is greater than the load. In activity 14 you will look at a system using a single pulley which does gain a mechanical advantage.

Activity 14

1 Set up this arrangement.

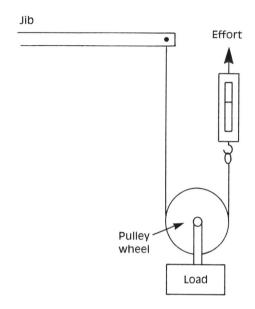

Raise the load by pulling up on the newton-meter. Read and record the amount of effort needed. Work out the mechanical advantage.

2 Repeat step 1, but this time measure the distances moved by the load and by the effort. Work out the velocity ratio.

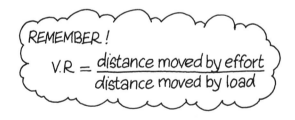

REMEMBER! V.R = distance moved by effort / distance moved by load

Although the system in activity 14 gains a mechanical advantage, it is difficult to use. It is easier to pull downwards than to pull upwards! Using a system with more than one pulley helps to solve this problem.

3.2 Pulley and belt systems

Pulley and belt systems are used to transmit rotary motion and force from one axle or shaft to another. They are used in automatic washing machines, car engines, pillar drills and in many other places.

Activity 15

Change the pulley system of activity 14 so that you raise the load by pulling downwards. Work out the mechanical advantage of your new system. Is it the same?

Activity 16

Design and make a pulley system using no more than 4 pulley wheels. Try to make the mechanical advantage gained as large as possible.

Optional work

If you use different sized pulley wheels, does it affect the mechanical advantage gained? What happens to the velocity ratio? Write down what you think first. Then try out different pulley systems to see if you were right.

Activity 17

1 Use a construction kit to make a pulley and belt system. Use different sized wheels.

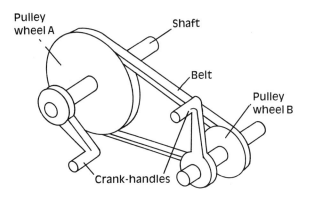

When you turn one wheel, the movement and force will be transmitted to the other wheel by the belt. The wheel that you turn is called the **driver** wheel. The other wheel is called the **driven** wheel.

2 Turn wheel A 10 times, and count how many times the driven wheel B turns. Work out the velocity ratio, like this.

$$V.R. = \frac{\text{Distance moved by driver wheel}}{\text{Distance moved by driven wheel}}$$

$$= \frac{10 \text{ revolutions}}{\text{Number of times wheel B turned}}$$

3 Turn wheel A, but try to prevent wheel B from turning by applying an opposing force on its crank-handle. What happens?

4 Sometimes the belt on a pulley and belt system is too slack. The system then fails to transmit movement and force because the belt slips.

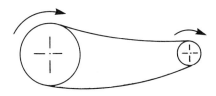

Design a way of overcoming this problem without changing the distance between the axles or shortening the belt.

5 Design a way of reversing the direction of the driven pulley.

Engineers have designed a number of ways of trying to prevent **slip** in pulley and belt systems. These include ways of **tensioning** (tightening) the belt, and improving the 'grip' of the belt on the wheels by changing the design of both. Look at the transmission system in a lathe or a pillar drill for examples of these.

3.3 Sprocket and chain systems

Sometimes a direct **positive drive** is essential, when there must be no slipping between the driver and the driven wheels. To guarantee against the possibility of slip, a **sprocket and chain** system can be used.

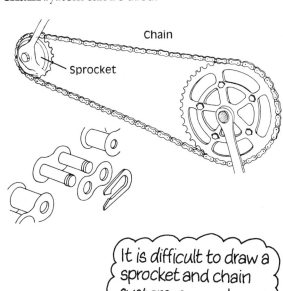

It is difficult to draw a sprocket and chain system, so people use this symbol.

Activity 18

1 Use a kit to construct a sprocket and chain system.

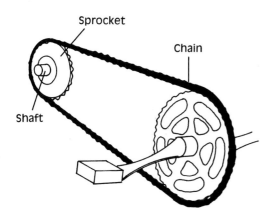

2 Turn the smaller sprocket 10 times. Count the number of turns the larger sprocket makes, and work out the velocity ratio for this system. (Use the method of activity 17 step 2.)

3 There is another way of finding the velocity ratio. Try to work out what it is.

It has something to do with the number of teeth on each sprocket.

Optional work

1 Look at two different bikes – one with derailler gears and the other with Sturmey Archer gears. Try to work out the velocity ratios of the various gear arrangements.

2 On the derailer gears, how is the length of the chain adjusted for the different gear arrangements?

76

4 Gears and gear mechanisms

4.1 Simple gear trains

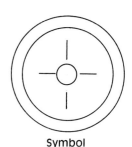

Gear-wheel   Symbol

A gear-wheel transmits rotary motion and force. It has accurately made teeth around its edge. When the teeth of one gear-wheel are interlocking with those of another, the gears are **meshing**. (Would gear-wheels with different sized teeth be able to mesh properly?)

The gear-wheels you will use in this section are **spur gears**. When two spur gears of different diameters mesh, the large gear is called the **wheel** and the smaller is the **pinion**. A system of gears meshing together is a **gear train**.

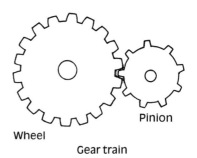

Wheel

Pinion

Gear train

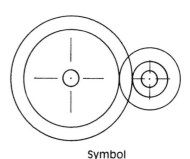

Symbol

Activity 19

1 Use a kit to construct a gear train. Add crank-handles to the axles.

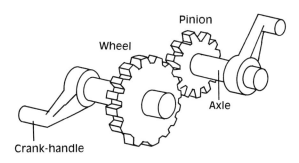

2 Turn the wheel gear (the **driver** gear) 10 times. Count how many times the pinion gear (the **driven** gear) turns. Work out the velocity ratio of the train like this:

$$V.R. = \frac{\text{Distance moved by driver wheel}}{\text{Distance moved by driven wheel}}$$

$$= \frac{10\,\text{turns}}{\text{Number of turns of driven gear}}$$

3 Turn the wheel gear again, but try to stop the pinion from turning by applying an opposing force through its crank-handle. Write down whether it was easy or hard to stop the driven wheel from turning.

4 Repeat steps 2 and 3, but use the pinion as the driver gear and the wheel as the driven gear.

Motion and force are transmitted through a gear train by the teeth of the driver gear **levering** the teeth of the driven gear around.

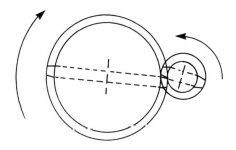

One result of this is that the direction of rotation is reversed. If the driver gear is turning in a clockwise direction, the driven gear will turn anticlockwise.

Activity 20

Try to modify the gear train of activity 19 so that the driver and driven gears both turn in the same direction.

If three gears are used in a gear train, the driver and driven gears both turn in the same direction. In this kind of train, the middle gear is called an **idler**.

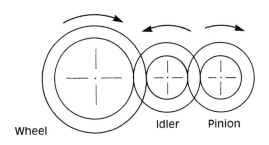

Activity 21

1 Construct a gear train like the one in the diagram overleaf. Use a large gear-wheel for the

idler. Turn the wheel gear 10 times, and count how many times the pinion turns. Work out the velocity ratio.

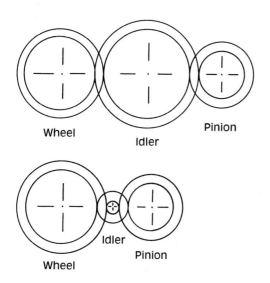

Wheel — Idler — Pinion

Wheel — Idler — Pinion

2 Replace the large idler gear with a smaller gear-wheel. Find the velocity ratio for this gear train.

3 Does changing the size of the idler gear affect the velocity ratio of the gear train?

Optional work

There is another way of working out the velocity ratio of a gear train. It has something to do with the number of teeth on the driver and driven wheels. Find out how to do it, then work out the velocity ratio of each of these trains.

1 Driver gear 19 teeth, driven gear 57 teeth

2 Driver gear 30 teeth, driven gear 60 teeth

3 Driver gear 60 teeth, driven gear 12 teeth

4.2 Compound gear trains

Simple gear trains can be used to gain a mechanical advantage or achieve a velocity ratio, but only to a limited extent. For example, if you use the largest wheel available in your kit to drive the smallest pinion, you can only achieve a velocity ratio of about 4. If a large velocity ratio is needed to solve a problem, a **compound** gear train is used.

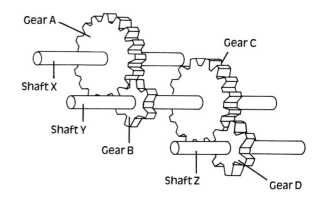

Compound gear train

A compound gear train combines two or more simple gear trains by making them share a common shaft. In the picture above, gears A and B form one gear train, and gears C and D the other. Shaft Y is common to both gear trains.

Activity 22

Construct a compound gear train similar to the one shown. You will need to work out how to support the shafts X, Y and Z so that they are parallel to each other and are held steady when force and motion is transmitted through the gear train. Two possible layouts are shown below.

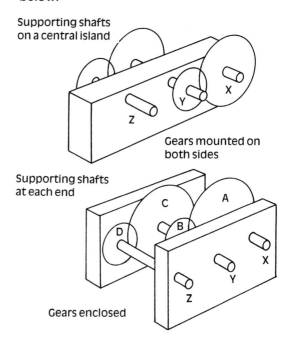

Supporting shafts on a central island

Gears mounted on both sides

Supporting shafts at each end

Gears enclosed

Use your compound gear train in activities 23 and 24.

Activity 23

In this activity you will find out what happens to the velocity ratio when a compound gear train is used (in other words, how the transmission of **motion** is affected).

1 Turn axle X through 10 revolutions, so that gear-wheel A is the driver gear. Count how many turns axle Z makes (the output). Work out the velocity ratio.

2 Now turn axle Z through 10 revolutions, so that the gear pinion is the driver gear. Count how many turns axle X makes. Work out the velocity ratio.

3 How does using the gear pinion as driver affect the output motion?

Activity 24

This activity looks at the way **force** is transmitted through a compound gear train.

1 Apply force and motion to axle X by steadily turning it. Try to prevent axle Z from turning by applying an opposing force to it. Write down whether it was easy or hard to stop the output shaft from turning.

2 Repeat step 1, but with axle Z as the input shaft and axle X the output shaft.

3 How does using the gear pinion as driver affect the output motion?

Optional work

How do the ideas shown by activities 23 and 24 link in with riding a bike with gears?

4.3 Going round corners

In all the gear trains you have made so far, the axle shafts have been **parallel** to one another. This is because the gear trains were made from spur gears.

Parallel shafts

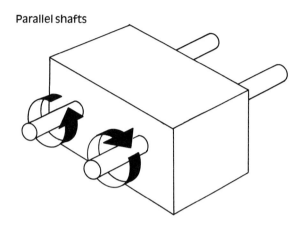

Sometimes engineers or designers need to use a gear system in which the axle shafts are at right-angles to one another. This section looks at some of the solutions to this problem.

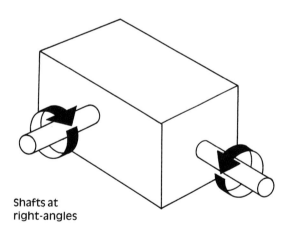

Shafts at right-angles

Bevel gears have teeth cut on a cone instead of a cylinder.

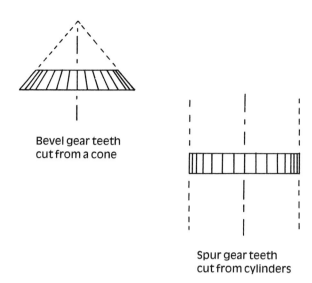

Bevel gear teeth cut from a cone

Spur gear teeth cut from cylinders

They are meshed together in pairs to transmit rotary motion and force between two shafts at right-angles to one another.

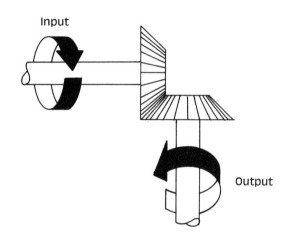

Input

Output

When the pair of meshed bevel gears have the same number of teeth (as in the picture above), they are called **mitre** gears.

Activity 25

1 Will mitre gears change the velocity of the output shaft compared to that of the input shaft? Write down what you think, then make a model to see if you were right.

2 Find an example of bevel gears in use. Does this example change the velocity between input and output?

Another solution to the problem of transmitting rotary motion between two shafts at right-angles to each other is to use a **worm gear**. The worm gear is a type of screw thread attached to an axle shaft. The worm meshes with a **worm-wheel** which is mounted on an axle at right-angles to the worm.

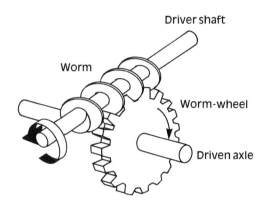

Driver shaft

Worm

Worm-wheel

Driven axle

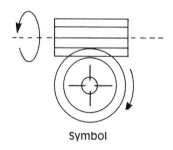

Symbol

The worm gear is often called the 'one-toothed gear' because it acts like a gear with a single tooth. Each time it makes a full revolution, it will only turn the worm-wheel through one tooth. If the worm-wheel has 30 teeth, the worm gear will have to turn 30 times for the worm-wheel to turn once. This means that a large reduction in velocity can be achieved by using a worm gear and worm-wheel.

4.4 Changing rotary motion to linear motion

All the gear systems you have looked at transmit a rotary input to a rotary output. The **rack and pinion** is different. It converts a rotary motion into a linear motion.

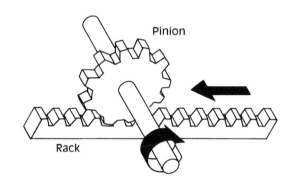

Pinion

Rack

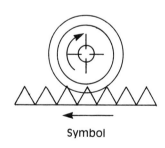

Symbol

Activity 26

1 Make a model meshing a worm gear with a suitable spur gear. Drive the worm gear through 10 revolutions by turning the worm axle shaft. Record the output revolutions of the spur gear.

2 Work out the velocity ratio. (You may need to use a greater number of input revolutions.)

3 Try to reverse the direction of transmission of force by driving the spur gear. **Do not force it!** Is it possible to have the worm gear as a **driven** gear?

81

Rack and pinion systems are sometimes used on mountain railways.

2 Design and make a vehicle which will travel a horizontal distance of 10 metres as quickly as possible.

3 Design and make a vehicle which can climb a steep slope and travel along a horizontal surface at speed. To do this you will need to design a gear-box with at least two speeds, so that the correct gear train can be used for each purpose.

4 Design and make a model of a system which could be used to get a rescue line from the shore to someone in difficulties in a rough sea. Your model needs to be able to do two things.
(a) It must be able to send a line accurately to the person in trouble (who, for your model, is 3 metres away).

Activity 27

1 Build a model of a rack and pinion system.

2 The rack and pinion can convert rotary motion into linear motion (and vice versa) in three different ways. Work out what these are. Modify the model you made in step 1 to show each of the different ways.

Design technology projects

1 Design and build a vehicle to climb very steep slopes. You are not allowed to attach anything to the slope – the vehicle must climb the slope under its own power.

(b) When the person is safely attached to the line, the system must be able to pull them safely to the shore with the minimum of effort (for your model, this means pulling in a load of 5 newtons with a minimum of effort).

5 Your parents are complaining that the family uses too many toilet rolls! Design and make a toilet roll holder which will only let a limited amount of paper go with each pull. It should be easy to reset the device after use – so that it is ready for the next customer!

6 Design and make a humane mousetrap. Your solution must be a ventilated container of some kind with a door which closes quickly when the mouse enters and 'triggers' the mechanism. Your solution must not hurt the mouse in any way, and the mechanism that closes the door must be easy to reset.

Mechanisms word search

```
M X W K V I E T C O K T Q I U E S P U L L E Y A L
M A C H I N E A E D F O T R E W Q U I O P K H E D
E M O D I F Z T H E P U O L L E Y A N D G E A R C
C R A T I O T H R O L I N K A G E U G H T H I E K
H G E I T R S T E N T R E L V T I O N S H O N P S
A S A D V A N P T A G E F R I C T I E O N L C A M
N R G E S T M E R D I T T E R K N G E A N T L O A
I N P U T E N Y A O B L E T H E A O U T G Q I N G
S G I S A B T S I C C M E K H T A N I G A L N D N
M E S I G I N E D T O K R O N T A T E T H E E M I
E S H I C H G W I B H L E A G D A N D F I S D H F
E R T O C H N I C W R I V T L I N E A R X O P S Y
T H L I N K C A F O F D U L V Y A N D O B S L E I
R E V E L H E A C T A I V I T I E S L A N Y A O N
V F T H F S E W O L R D S A R E O M O T I O N B G
O U T P U T V I A O E U S O N E P R E S U L E T B
O R D O P N G C T H I V S W O R U D S R E A R C E
I S T O H E I L P Y O U E R A C L C U O R A T E A
M E M O R N I S C R E W I R T I L O N T O F S O M
M E O F A T H E T A R M I G O L E O G A T L O I K
A T Y H O U R B I C Y K L E A N Y D M R O T I R L
C A C R T O F S N D E X A L P L G E A Y E S O F O
M E C H A N I C A L E F F I C I E N C Y T H E O A
M E R A I L L E R O S C I L D A T V N G M O T I D
L O N D R A Y N G R S P H I C A L B Y E F F O R T
```

MECHANICAL ADVANTAGE
MACHINE
LEVER
INPUT
OUTPUT
INCLINED PLANE
SCREW
MOTION
LINKAGE
ROTARY
SPROCKET
LINEAR
GEAR
PULLEY
EFFORT
LOAD
EFFICIENCY

Find the following terms and words in this study of mechanisms e.g. MECHANISM is done for you.

Appendix 1 Electronics baseboard

The circuit baseboard used throughout Part 2 is based on the plan shown below. The positions of the spring-type junctions are important to allow easy fitting of components.

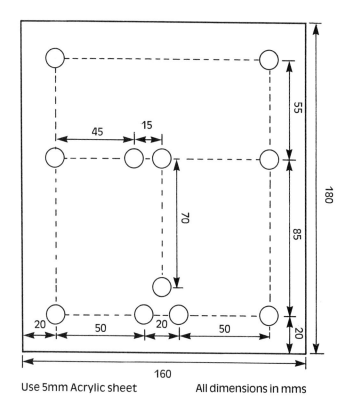

Use 5mm Acrylic sheet   All dimensions in mms

Appendix 2   Component sources

The following companies may be able to supply some or all of the materials and components which pupils need in order to participate in the practical learning activities in this book.

Educational construction kits

Kits such as Lego Technic Sets, Fischer Technik Sets, Meccano, and Electronics kits may be obtained from the following sources.

Commotion Technology Supplies, 241 Green Street, Enfield. 01–804–1378

Ely Resource Centre, Back Hill, Ely, Cambs. Please note that a full electronics kit especially designed for this book is supplied.

Economatics (Education) Ltd., Epic House, 9 Orgreave Road, Sheffield.   0742–690801

Nottingham Educational Supplies, 17 Ludlow Hill Road, West Bridgford, Nottingham.   0602–235922

Technology Teaching Systems, Penmore House, Hasland Road, Hasland, Chesterfield.   0246–78993

Electronics Components

JPR Electronics, Unit M, Kingsway Industrial Estate, Kingsway, Luton, Bedfordshire.   0582–410055

Rapid Electronics, Hill Farm Industrial Estate, Boxted, Colchester, Essex.   0206–36730

RS Components. Several U.K. locations, general enquiries to 0536–201234

STC Electronic Services, Edinburgh Way, Harlow, Essex.   0279–26811

Various components

Items such as motors, springs, magnets, fastening devices, switches, wheels etc., may be obtained from the following sources.

British Thorton (First steps project) P.O. Box 3, Wythenshawe, Manchester.   061–998–1311

Proops Distributors Ltd., Heybridge Estate, Castle Road, London NW1.   01–267–1718

K.R. Whiston Ltd., New Mills, Stockport.   0663–42028

Appendix 3　Basic electronics kit check list

1 set of PP9 battery press studs
4 croc-clips on flying leads
2 lamp holders (MES batten)
2 lamps 6V 60mA
1 rocker switch SP on/off
1 reed switch (normally open)
1 4.7 Ω resistor 0.5W carbon
1 33 Ω resistor 0.5W carbon
1 47 Ω resistor 0.5W carbon
1 56 Ω resistor 0.5W carbon
1 68 Ω resistor 0.5W carbon
1 330 Ω resistor 0.5W carbon
1 1k Ω resistor 0.5W carbon
1 15k Ω resistor 0.5W carbon
1 500 Ω variable resistor
1 10k Ω variable resistor
1 100k Ω variable resistor
1 diode OA 202 or IN4001
1 light dependent resistor ORP 12
1 thermistor TH3 TDR
1 transistor BFY51 or 2N3053
1 100µf capacitor 16V
1 470µf capacitor 16V
1 6–9V electric motor
1 6–12V buzzer
1 20mm × 20mm stripboard
1 m of 22 gauge black insulated wire 0.6mm
1 m of 22 gauge red insulated wire 0.6mm
1 baseboard drilled ready for springs
11 springs for baseboard
11 screws for fixing springs to baseboard

These items are available as a kit, if required, from The Ely Resource Centre, Back Hill, Ely, Cambridgeshire.

Further reading

Control Technology, (Pupils' Assignments and Teacher's Handbook), S.C.D.C., Hodder & Stoughton, (1978).

Design & Technology, 2nd ed. Yarwood, A., and Orme, H., Hodder & Stoughton, (1986).

Electronics for Today and Tomorrow, Duncan, T., John Murray, (1985).

Gears & Gearing, (Science at Work Series), Longman, (1985).

How Things Work, Volumes 1 & 2, Paladin, (1972, 74).

Modular Courses in Technology: Electronics, Energy resources, Mechanisms, Structures, S.C.D.C. Oliver & Boyd, (1980, 81, 82)

Technology & Production, Clews, G. and Leonard, R., Philip Alan, (1985).

Technology in School, Cave, J., Routledge, (1982).

The Engineering Design Process, Hawkes, B., and Abinett, R., Pitman, (1984).

The Robot Book, Pauson, R., Windward, (1984).

Solar Prospects, Flood, M., Wildwood House, (1983).